Hayden Computer Programming Series

The BASIC Workbook

CREATIVE TECHNIQUES FOR BEGINNING PROGRAMMERS

KENNETH SCHOMAN, JR.

Softech, Inc.
Former Chairman, Department of Mathematics,
Wilbraham and Monson Academy

HAYDEN BOOK COMPANY, INC.
Rochelle Park, New Jersey

Library of Congress Cataloging in Publication Data

Schoman, Kenneth.
  The BASIC workbook.

  (Hayden computer programming series)
  Includes index.
  1. Basic (Computer program language)
I. Title.
QA76.73.B3S36   001.6'424   77-3209
ISBN 0-8104-5104-2

5	6	7	8	9		PRINTING
78	79	80	81	82	83	84	85	YEAR

Preface

BASIC is a high-level programming language that can be used in a wide variety of applications. In an educational context, however, it is more than just another computer language. It is often the first one that students encounter. For this reason, an introductory course in programming must go beyond the language itself. Such a course should impart an appreciation for the art of programming since most students are not likely to look upon programming as an end in itself but rather just as a tool for solving problems.

This book is about programming in a BASIC environment. Because only twenty keywords are introduced, it is not really a BASIC text. With this limited vocabulary, however, one can do many things. What matters is that one recognize how a language can be used to build workable algorithms. Such knowledge is always useful, no matter what the language, the device, or the problem at hand.

The curriculum which spawned this book emphasized the algorithmic nature of problem solving. The object of the course was to put BASIC into operation effectively, which meant working with at least high school upperclassmen (although some sophomores did enroll). It covered simple elements of programming style, and it encouraged discovery rather than exposition. For anyone who had an idea and wondered if it would work, the maxim was: "There's only one way to find out. Try it!"

This book began as a graded collection of problems. Relatively unstructured, they are not mere modifications of text examples but rather valid computer applications of increasing difficulty. Requiring both creativity and discipline, they provide a healthy set of tasks for a ten- to fifteen-week term. The exercises have been supplemented with a limited series of lectures and many leading questions. Nearly a hundred students worked with the material over a two-year period. They were largely high school juniors and seniors, and college freshmen. Because they wanted to listen without the interference of taking notes, the text evolved.

As may be obvious, the text is an expanded series of lecture notes. It is meant more to summarize than to explain. Topics peculiar to BASIC, not within most secondary school curricula, or beyond the capabilities of many school computer systems, are omitted.

Wherever possible, the book is consistent with, but not limited by, ANSI draft standards for minimal BASIC. The book may be used with a wide variety of computer systems (the author used four different systems while preparing the examples and problems).

Since BASIC is an interactive language, the author assumes that programs will be executed at an appropriate terminal producing printed output. If a special login procedure is needed, directions must be given with the "First Day" exercise. Also useful are instructions for saving lengthy programs on tape or disk. Throughout the book, discussions of particular implementations are minimized.

No text can be developed without the generous help of experts and readers alike. The assistance of three people made the publication of this book possible. They are F. Arthur Tuttle, former Headmaster of Wilbraham & Monson Academy, Anthony DiCenzo of Digital Equipment Corporation, and Dianne Littwin of Hayden Book Company

Many others commented on the manuscript, worked on the program at Wilbraham & Monson, or gave needed advice at critical points along the way. These contributors include Dr. Richard Brown, Marianne Büttner, Dr. George Caruso, Tim Flint, Hugh Harrell, Reuben Jones, Walter Koetke, Henry LaFleur, Robert Valentine, Herb Wilkinson, and Barry Wolman. And, of course, the author must extend his thanks to all the students who enrolled in programming courses at Wilbraham & Monson. Their contributions were immeasurable.

KENNETH SCHOMAN, JR.

Contents

## Chapter 1

Computers and Problem Solving

Computers are calculating machines in which information, including instructions, can be stored and manipulated. Scientists and engineers employ the machine's accuracy and speed to perform complex mathematical calculations. Businesses depend on the computer's ability to hold and organize large amounts of information.

Computers are as useful for doing simple tasks many times as they are for solving complicated problems. A computer will do nothing, however, until it is given instructions. And a computer does exactly what it is instructed to do (even if the instructions are faulty). Writing instructions for a computer is called "programming." To use a computer, you do not need to know very much about how it works. In that sense, programming is like cooking. Almost everyone can use or write a recipe without knowing about chemical reactions.

When you tell a computer what to do, you must know how to solve the problem at hand. The computer merely saves you time and effort in carrying out all the steps. Simple problems that can be solved by hand should not be worked out on a computer. And complicated problems that can be made simple by using the proper mathematics should be solved that way. Like mathematics itself, a computer is a tool to help people solve problems.

Problem solving

This book will help you learn about computer programming. In addition, it is hoped that your discoveries will make you a better problem solver. Problem solving is not just finding an answer. It is determining what steps must be performed in order to reach a solution.

To be a good problem solver, you must ask yourself, before doing any other work, what will the answer look like? Will it be a picture, a number, or a set or words? Roughly how big will it be? How many different outcomes are possible? Could they occur all together or only one at a time? What will decide which answer belongs to this particular problem? How long must you work on this problem before you decide that your answer is good enough?

Teachers can tell you how to write your solu-

tions so that a computer will understand them. But teachers cannot tell you "the answer" to most of the problems in this book. There is no single answer. Your solution is yours alone.

Writing instructions

Many of the problems in this book begin with the words, "Write a program which will . . . ." A program is a set of instructions telling how to perform a task, solve a problem, or play a game. Such a set of instructions may also be called an "algorithm."

A computer program is one written in a language that a computer can understand. A program does not have to be a computer program. Any language may be used. For example, suppose you wrote the following:

STARTING A CAR

1. Enter car, key in hand.
2. Insert key in ignition.
3. Fasten safety belt.
4. Put gearshift in neutral.
5. Depress gas pedal.
6. Turn key.
7. If engine starts, release key; otherwise, see "What To Do If Motor Fails"
8. End of instructions.

This program is written in plain English, but it has several features in common with computer programs:

1. It is a set of instructions which tells how to perform a task.
2. The instructions must be performed in a certain sequence.
3. The program allows for more than one outcome.
4. One instruction indicates the end of the program.
5. Whoever performs the task must recognize certain objects (the key, the gearshift, and so forth).

Note that we have not really started the car. We have merely explained how it is to be done.

The problems in this book are to be treated in the same way. You should first decide how to go about each and write a set of instructions. Then, you can use a computer to execute your program and solve the problem.

Using the computer

The problems in this book do not require advanced mathematics. They do require lots of good thinking on your part. You will learn computer programming only if you work on the problems yourself, at least one from each chapter. You will not learn by copying someone else's solution. If at first you cannot do a problem, don't quit. Ask for help. Anyone offering it should ask only those questions which will lead you to your own solution.

The exercise at the end of this chapter will demonstrate a form of simple programming that is suitable for your first day at the computer. Throughout the book, all programs will be written in BASIC, which is just one of many languages for writing computer programs.

You will use the computer by typing your instructions on the keyboard of a computer terminal. This looks like a fancy typewriter. On many keys, there are two symbols. To type the lower symbol, just press the key. To type the upper symbol, hold the SHIFT key down and press the symbol key. The unmarked bar at the bottom of the keyboard produces spaces.

Press the RETURN or CR key at the end of every line you type.

Note that there is a difference between the letter "O" and the number zero. In this book, the zero key is indicated by $\emptyset$. Your computer may slash the letter O instead or show the difference some other way.

Don't be afraid of pressing the wrong key. It won't hurt anything. If you make a mistake, you can "erase" the character just typed by typing a back arrow, ← (this is either the SHIFT/O or RUB-OUT key). To erase two letters, type ← ←, and so forth. For example, RS←EM will be understood by the computer as REM.

For now, ignore any other buttons attached to the terminal.

Before using the computer, you may have to "log in" (following a procedure described by your teacher or by the manufacturer of the computer).

All set? Read on . . . .

Exercise for the first day

Read this whole exercise carefully before working at the computer. If you do so, it can be done in about 40 minutes. To begin, type your name and press the RETURN key. The computer will respond with WHAT? or ??? or ERROR or some similar response to indicate that it did not understand what you told it. Since we must give language that the computer understands, we type either

SCRATCH

SCR or NEW

and press RETURN again. Most computers understand one of these commands, but not both. Either command will erase any previous instructions left in the machine. The computer should respond by printing READY, or by advancing the paper so you can type on the next line (this is called a "line-feed"), or by asking for a program name (give it any name and press RETURN again). Now type the following:

```
       variable
10 LET X=999
20 PRINT X
30 END
```

This is a program. It has three instructions or "statements," one to a line. Each line is numbered ($1\emptyset$, $2\emptyset$, $3\emptyset$) to form a sequence. By being typed, this program is stored in the computer's memory. To prove this to yourself, ask the computer to print what is in its memory. Type

LIST

Then ask the computer to carry out your instructions by typing

RUN

The LET statement will be used to do most calculations. The program above assigns the value 999 to the variable X, then prints the value of X. If we decide to assign another value to that variable, the previous one is wiped out. Let's assign, in order, a sum, a difference, a product, a quotient, and a number raised to a power. To erase the first program, type

SCR or NEW

Now type a new program:

```
10 LET X=2+3
20 PRINT X
30 LET X=2-3
40 PRINT X
50 LET X=2*3
60 PRINT X
70 LET X=2/3
80 PRINT X
```

```
 90 LET X=2↑3
100 PRINT X
110 END
```

Execute the program by typing:

RUN

Note that computer language is a little different from ordinary math. An "asterisk" is used to multiply, and the symbol for "raising to a power" is usually ↑ (and sometimes ∧). Where we would write 2x3 in mathematics, we type 2*3 for the computer. And instead of 2^3, we now type 2↑3.

The LET statement is usually used for doing calculations, but the PRINT statement can handle them also. With PRINT, more than one expression can be put on a line if they are separated by commas or semicolons. And the computer will skip a line if it is asked to PRINT nothing. Try the following program (do not forget to type SCR or NEW before and RUN after):

```
10 PRINT
20 PRINT 2+3, 2-3, 2*3, 2/3, 2↑3
30 PRINT
40 PRINT 2+3; 2-3; 2*3; 2/3; 2↑3
50 END
```

What is the difference between a comma and a semicolon?

Messages will be printed if they are enclosed in quotes. Try this:

```
10 PRINT "SUM OF TWO NUMBERS"
20 LET X=3
30 LET Y=4
40 PRINT "3+4=": X+Y
50 END
```

What if we wanted to write a program like the last one except that we desire to add two numbers *which we would supply later*? Try this:

```
10 PRINT "SUM OF TWO NUMBERS"
20 INPUT X
30 INPUT Y
40 PRINT "3+4="; X+Y
50 END
```

When we run this program, the computer will type a question mark. The machine is asking for the value of X. Therefore, type 3 right after the question mark, as follows:

?3

and press RETURN. Then the computer will ask for Y. Input 4, as follows:

?4

and press RETURN. Your whole run should look like this:

```
RUN
SUM OF TWO NUMBERS
?3
?4
3+4= 7
```

Note that if we gave the computer 5 when it asked for the value of X, and 6 when it asked for the value of Y, the computer would print on the last line

3+4= 11

That mistake would be our fault, not the machine's.

As a final exercise, type and run the following program. It will be discussed in the next chapter.

```
10 LET X=.0000001
20 PRINT X
30 LET X=X*10
40 IF X<100000000 THEN 20
50 PRINT
60 PRINT "AGENT", 0; 0; (25+3)/4
70 PRINT
80 END
```

Chapter 2
Elementary Statements

A program written in BASIC is a list of instructions or "statements," one statement to a line. Each line is numbered. The computer executes the statements in sequence. In the "First Day" exercise, we used five program statements: END, LET, PRINT, INPUT, and IF-THEN. More will be said about these shortly.

We also used three kinds of "system commands": NEW or SCR, LIST, and RUN. These are also instructions to the computer. However, they are not numbered, are not used in programs, and are executed as soon as they are typed in.

System commands

Every computer has at least three parts (see Fig. 2-1). It has devices for putting information into the machine and getting results out (input/output, or I/O devices). It has a device for executing instructions (the central processing unit, or CPU). And it has a device for storing information (the memory). An input/output device will be called a "terminal." The most common form of memory is called "core" because it is made of small magnetic rings or cores woven together with threads of wire. Most computers have other kinds of memory as well and several input/output devices. In general, though, all computers have the three kinds of equipment mentioned.

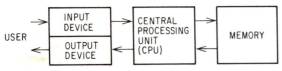

Fig. 2-1. Schematic diagram of computer system

System commands are direct instructions to the CPU. The three commands we have used are interpreted by the CPU to mean the following things:

1. LIST: Type at the terminal all statements now stored in memory.
2. RUN: Execute all statements now stored in memory, starting with the lowest numbered and stopping when instructed to do so.

3. NEW or SCR: Erase (scratch) all statements now stored in memory.

If you are working at one of several terminals attached to the same computer (known as "time-sharing"), these commands affect only that portion of the memory assigned to your terminal. After typing NEW or SCR, the computer's list of stored instructions will be empty. To have the computer work for us, we must type a program into the machine, then tell it to execute the statements.

Fundamental quantities

Before discussing program statements, we need to define a few terms:

1. "Constant": For now, a constant is any specific number.
2. "Variable": For now, a variable can be any one of the 26 letters (such as "X"), or one letter and one digit (such as "X2").
3. "Operation": Operations are add (+), subtract (−), multiply (*), divide (/), and raise to a power (either ↑ or ∧).
4. "Expression": An expression is any combination of constants and/or variables, separated by operations. Parentheses may be used. An expression does not include an equals sign. Examples of expressions are:

   3
   M
   X+8
   2*(K−4.59)

5. "Line number": Line numbers must be integers. They will be designated by the symbol #.

Program statements

Examples of all following program statements can be found in the "First Day" exercise (Chap. 1).

The END statement has a higher number than any other line. It instructs the computer to stop executing the current program.

\# END

Last statement of program.

Think of the computer's memory as a pigeon-hole mailbox. Each pigeonhole is named by a variable and can hold one number. The LET statement computes the value of the expression and assigns that value to the pigeonhole named by the variable.

LET variable = expression

Assign value of expression to variable.

The LET statement must have the format shown above, or the computer will not understand it. It is not the same as an equation. For example, LET 2*C–32 = B will not work because the variable and expression are reversed.

The statement LET X = X*10 will work. To the CPU, it means: Get the number stored in place X, multiply it by ten, and store the result in place X. When this is done, the number that was in X at the beginning has disappeared. Since the variable X can have only one value at a time, the original number has been replaced by one ten times as large.

Before a program is run, the number stored in every variable (on most machines) is zero. (Since this is not always the case, you may have to "initialize" some variables to zero at the beginning of a program.)

Remember the difference between an expression, which always reflects some mathematical value, and text:

PRINT X means print the value of variable X
PRINT "X" means print the letter "X"

Several expressions, or a combination of expressions and texts, may appear in a PRINT statement.

PRINT expression, expression, . . .
PRINT "text"
PRINT

Print values of expressions and specified text. Spacing is controlled by comma and semicolon.

The comma and semicolon are known as "separators." A comma acts as if the page were divided into columns. Each zone is at least 14 spaces wide (depending on the computer). Every time a comma is used in PRINT, the typing head moves to the next zone. A semicolon means "print close together."

It is a good idea to use LET for all calculations and to use PRINT only for reporting results. Adopting this habit will make your programming knowledge useful in other computer languages.

An INPUT statement will accept more than one value if the variables are separated by commas. If more than one number is requested by an INPUT statement, the values may be typed on one line provided that they, too, be separated by commas.

INPUT variable, variable, . . .

Get values of variables from keyboard.

If the computer encounters an INPUT statement when executing a program, it will print a question mark (called an "input prompt") and will wait for the user to type the needed numbers. Numbers supplied by the user may also be called "data."

Although it may look complicated, the IF statement is not hard to understand.

IF expression relation expression
THEN line-number

If the relation between the values of the expressions is true, then continue execution at the line-number. If the relation is false, then proceed to the line numerically after this one.

The relations that may be used in an IF statement are as follows:

<	less than
< =	less than or equal to
=	equal to
> =	greater than or equal to
>	greater than
< >	not equal to

For example, the last program of the "First Day" exercise was

```
10 LET X=.0000001
20 PRINT X
30 LET X=X*10
40 IF X<100000000 THEN 20
50 PRINT
60 PRINT "AGENT", 0; 0; (25+3)/4
70 PRINT
80 END
```

Note that the lines are numbered in differences of ten. This is merely good programming practice. If

Elementary Statements

space is left between consecutive line numbers, there will later be room to insert statements that may have been forgotten.

It should be obvious that the program returns from line 40 to line 20 many times. How many times? Until line 30 assigns the value 100 million to X. Then the relation stated in line 40 will be false. When this happens, the computer goes on to line 50.

When this program is run, we would expect to see the machine start printing the following:

```
.0000001
.000001
.00001
.0001
```

But this is not what happens. We actually see something like this:

```
1.0000E-7
1.0000E-6
.00001
.0001
```

What happened? The computer expresses very small or very large numbers in "scientific notation." The number 1.0000E+6 is the computer's way of writing 1×10^6, or one million. The "E" stands for "exponent" or "times ten raised to the power" and is followed by another number representing that power in positive or negative terms. Thus, E-6 stands for 1×10^{-6}.

Order of operations

Note the use of parentheses in the program:

```
50 PRINT
60 PRINT "AGENT", 0; 0; (25+3)/4
70 PRINT
80 END
```

What if the parentheses were omitted? Would the expression 25+3/4 be interpreted as $\frac{25+3}{4}$ or as $25 + \frac{3}{4}$? Since expressions are written on a single line, we need to know the order in which operations are carried out.

In accordance with the order given in the box in the right-hand column, 25+3/4 is evaluated as 25.75, and (25+3)/4 is evaluated as 7.

Just for exercise, how is $2\uparrow2*3+4/2$ evaluated? Step-by-step, it becomes $4*3+4/2$, then $12+4/2$, then $12+2$, and finally 14. How is $8+16/2\uparrow2+4*1/2$ evaluated? The answer is, again, 14. As you can see, each of these expressions is hard to decipher.

An expression is evaluated as follows:

First	( )	expressions inside parentheses
Then	$\uparrow$	raising to a power
Next	* /	multiply and divide (from left to right)
Last	+ −	add and subtract (from left to right)

Therefore, use parentheses for clarity, even if they are not needed mathematically.

To establish proper order, parentheses may be used within parentheses. For example, the expression $(2*(3+1))\uparrow2$ has the value 64.

Solving the problems in this book

At this point, we know five program statements: END, LET, PRINT, INPUT, and IF-THEN. To solve a problem, statements need only be put together in the proper sequence, like a jigsaw puzzle. There will always be more than one way to solve every problem, however.

For example, suppose we want to write a program which will add any two numbers and print their sum. There is more than one program which will do this. To find out if a program works, run it. You will find, for example, that the following program works:

```
10 INPUT A,B
20 PRINT "SUM = "; A+B
30 END

RUN

?3,4
SUM =  7

READY
```

The following program also works:

```
10 INPUT A
20 INPUT B
30 LET S=A+B
40 PRINT "SUM = "; S
50 END

RUN

?3
```

```
?4
SUM =  7
```

```
READY
```

Do not try for a perfect solution right off. At first, you may get a solution which does the job but is awkward, or one which is only a partial solution. As you work on it, your solution will become more elegant. This process of trial-and-error is quite natural and is to be expected.

If you become stuck, try doing a simpler version of the problem; then expand that. *Experiment.* And seek advice when it is needed.

If your program uses INPUT, test it by using simple numbers. These should be numbers for which you know the answer. When you know that the program works, then you can input any numbers.

Problems

HYPOTENUSE

Write a program which will compute the hypotenuse of any right triangle, given the lengths of the legs.

NOTES: By the Pythagorean theorem, if the two legs of a right triangle are A and B and the hypotenuse is C, then:

$$C^2 = A^2 + B^2$$

The variables A and B may be called "parameters." A parameter is a variable that may take on any value. You do not need to know what the lengths of the legs are when you write the program. The lengths may just be represented by A and B. Later, when the program is executed, any lengths may be given if the program is written properly. To find a square root, remember that

$$\sqrt{x} = x^{\frac{1}{2}}.$$

POWERS AND ROOTS

List the integers from 1 to 20, their squares, their cubes, their square roots, and their cube roots in a table of five nicely spaced columns. Label the columns appropriately.

WEIGHT IN SPACE

Write a program which will ask the user his or her weight, then print the equivalent weight on each of the planets in the solar system and on the moon.

NOTES: The ratio of an object's weight on each of the planets to its weight on earth is:

Mercury	*0.27*
Venus	*0.85*
Earth	*1.00*
Moon	*0.16*
Mars	*0.38*
Jupiter	*2.64*
Saturn	*1.17*
Uranus	*0.92*
Neptune	*1.12*
Pluto	*Unknown*

These are sometimes called "gravity ratios." Because of them, as an example, astronauts going to the moon must have heavy boots to help them cope with their loss of weight, since a man on the moon weighs only 16 percent of what he does on earth.

MILEAGE

Assume you normally drive about 10,000 miles per year. You are about to buy an automobile and have seen EPA mileage ratings ranging from 10 miles per gallon (mpg) for a heavy luxury car to 40 mpg for a small economy sedan. Write a program which will list, in three columns, miles per gallon from 10 to 40, how many gallons of gasoline will be used in one year, and how much that gasoline will cost.

NOTES: To write this program, you will need to know the approximate price of regular grade gasoline in cents per gallon.

SIMPLY MULTIPLYING

Write a program which will multiply two binomials, (Mx + P) and (Nx + T), when given any values of M, P, N, and T. The result must be printed in the form,

$$Ax^2 + Bx + C$$

NOTES: The variables M, N, P, and T may be called "parameters." A parameter is a variable which may take on any arbitrary value. Specific values are chosen only after the program has been executed, not when it is being written.

Chapter 3
The Art of Programming

Solving a problem on a computer involves several stages of activity for the programmer. First you must *design a program* which will solve the problem at hand. Then you have to *write the program* in a manner that other people (as well as the computer) can understand. Last, you must *test the program* on the machine to make sure it works properly. And of course, you must fix it if it does not work. In each of these stages, a few suggestions can make your job easier.

Designing programs

It is a good idea to draw a diagram of your solution before writing a program. Such diagrams, called "flowcharts," consist mainly of boxes (showing operations to be performed) and arrows (showing the path from step to step). For example, to "add any two numbers and print their sum," the diagram in Fig. 3-1 might be drawn.

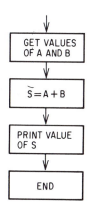

Fig. 3-1. Sum of two numbers

People who work with flowcharts use many different shapes to represent different operations. In this book, we will depart from the usual practice. We will use only two shapes (Fig. 3-2). A diamond will represent a question or decision. It will result in an IF-THEN statement. A box will represent everything else.

To sketch out solutions to problems, you do not even have to use the diamond shape. Just using boxes (and arrows) to represent all operations can be helpful. The words inside the boxes should re-

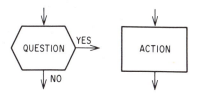

Fig. 3-2. Flowchart shapes

flect your general thinking. They need not be statements.

As an example, suppose you need a table to convert American dollars into Italian lira. Assume that the rate of exchange is $1.00 for 627 lira and that the amounts run from 10 cents to $2.00 in differences of 10 cents. The flowchart in Fig. 3-3 shows one way to carry out this assignment. From the flowchart, the following program was written easily:

```
10 PRINT "DOLLARS", "LIRA"
20 LET D=.10
30 LET L=D*627
```

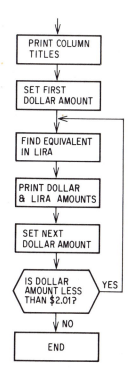

Fig. 3-3. Conversion flowchart

13

```
40 PRINT D,L
50 LET D=D+.10
60 IF D<2.01 THEN 30
70 END
```

This program contains a "loop" where the IF–THEN statement directs the computer to go back to an earlier statement. An IF–THEN statement is represented in a flowchart by a question. If the answer to that question is "YES," the IF–THEN returns the computer to an earlier statement in the program. For this reason, an IF–THEN statement is known as a "conditional transfer."

Another function of IF–THEN is to select which of two operations should be performed. For example, suppose you want a very simple program which, when given any two numbers, will tell if those numbers are equal. Such a program is shown in Fig. 3–4.

If the answer to the question is "YES," the flowchart shows that the program skips the "UNEQUAL" box and prints "EQUAL." If the answer to the question is "NO," the program goes to the box just after the question and prints "UNEQUAL."

Suppose that the answer to the question is "NO" and that the program prints "UNEQUAL." When it has done that, we want it to skip over the "equal" box, as shown by the dotted line. But this action cannot be programmed with any of the statements we know so far. For example, the program below will not do it:

```
10 PRINT "TO TEST EQUALITY,"
20 PRINT "INPUT TWO NUMBERS"
30 INPUT A,B
40 IF A=B THEN 60
50 PRINT "UNEQUAL"
60 PRINT "EQUAL"
70 END
```

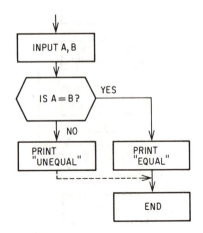

Fig. 3–4. Test for equality of two numbers

We need a statement between lines 50 and 60 which will cause the computer to skip line 60 every time. There is no decision involved. We need what is called an "unconditional transfer." Such a transfer is effected by the GOTO statement.

GOTO line-number

Continue execution starting at line-number.

When a program is run, the computer executes its statements in numerical order unless instructed to do otherwise. A GOTO statement changes the order of execution every time it is encountered. Therefore, our example should contain the line

55 GOTO 70

Despite the usefulness of the GOTO statement, however, it should be used to change a sequence only where necessary. The IF–THEN should be used as much as possible.

You can now test your knowledge of flowcharts and program statements. Write a program which, when given any two numbers, will tell if they are equal, and if they are not, will tell which is larger.

Writing programs

After obtaining a program that appears to work, review it for neatness. It must be capable of being understood by the person who runs it (the user) and by the person who lists it (another programmer).

To help the user, insert PRINT statements with messages. For example, if a program has stored the length of a hypotenuse in C, the easiest way to print it would be as follows:

PRINT C

but a better way to do it would be

PRINT "THE HYPOTENUSE IS "; C

since a value is meaningless unless it is identified. Our goal in programming should be that shown in the box.

A person who knows nothing about a program should be able to sit at a terminal, type RUN, and use that program without any help from the programmer.

Toward this end, you must ask yourself, "What do I want the computer to print?" Then you must separate your messages from the results of calculations. For example, suppose you want to display the equation of a straight line, Y = MX + B, after computing its slope, M, and its Y-intercept, B. What do you want the computer to print?

Y = (   )*X + (   )

Value of   Value of
variable M   variable B

In this line, there will be two numbers, which are the values of M and B. There are also three messages (or texts), which are

"Y = ("   and   ")*X + ("   and   ")"

So the PRINT statement should be

```
# PRINT "Y = ("; M; ")*X + ("; B; ")"
```

Other messages to the user may include a brief description of what the program does, and, if it uses an INPUT statement, what data is required in response to a question mark.

As a rule, messages in PRINT statements should be enough to explain a program to other programmers, too. But occasionally you will want to explain how a program works in more detail. These comments may just be reminders to yourself. But whatever they are, you may decide not to burden the user with them. So there is a statement for these comments, called a REM statement, which will be useful only when a program is listed.

```
# REM text

Comment inserted in a program.
```

The text of a REM (for REMARK) statement will not be printed when a program is run. In other words, the REM line will be completely ignored when the computer executes the program. REM statements are most useful in longer programs, reminding you of what each part does. Moreover, the name REM alone (with no text) can be used to create visual space between different sections of a program.

REM statements are also good for stating the quantity a variable represents. Your program will be easier to read if you choose variable names that have something in common with the quantities they represent. For example, choose "S" for sum, "T" for tax, and so forth.

Testing programs

Program errors are known as "bugs," and fixing them is called "debugging" the program. Before running a program, you may want to check it on paper with one or two simple cases. Work through it yourself as though you were the computer. After all, a solution should work whether done by machine or by hand.

This "desk checking" may uncover some errors. Even if it does not, it will tell you what to expect when the machine does the work. Always look at answers given by the computer and ask yourself, "Are these reasonable results?" You should recognize whether the results are close enough to what you would expect or way off. Be suspicious. Never accept everything coming out of the machine as correct.

Whether tests are done by hand or on the machine, the number of tests does not matter. What does matter is that different cases be tested. Your goal is described in the box.

All valid input data should yield correct results.

All unacceptable input data should produce error messages (cleverly provided in PRINT statements). Do not assume that the user will always supply reasonable data.

For example, suppose we have written a program which will tell whether a triangle is a right triangle, an acute triangle, or an obtuse triangle. The program must be given the lengths of the sides of the triangle, the largest side last. What data should be used to test this program? Try the following values:

3,4,5	If the program correctly identifies this right triangle, it should identify them all.
2,4,5	An acute triangle.
1,4,5	The program should correctly identify this.
0,4,5	And this, too.
3,4,6	An obtuse triangle.
3,4,8	This should produce an error message.
4,5,3	The program should respond to all mistakes.
0,0,0	Even obvious ones.

During testing, be careful that changes made to fix errors do not themselves introduce new errors.

The Art of Programming

Problems

TEMPERATURES

Print the centigrade equivalents of all Fahrenheit temperatures from 0 to 250 degrees in differences of ten degrees.

NOTES: *If C is a temperature in centigrade and F is the same temperature in Fahrenheit, then*

$$C = \frac{5}{9} (F - 32)$$

PICKING THE LARGEST

Write a program which, when given any sequence of positive numbers, will print the largest number and its position in the list. The program should also print the number of items in the sequence.

NOTES: You will have to make up some lists of numbers to test the program. Let the last item always be 999999 to indicate the end of the sequence. This value is not to be included in the count of items in the list. Will your program work if there are no numbers in the list (the only entry being 999999)? What if the largest number appears more than once in the list?

TELLING TRIANGLES

Write a program which, when given the lengths of the sides of a triangle, will tell whether it is a right triangle, an acute triangle, or an obtuse triangle.

NOTES: You may want to refer to the earlier problem which computed the hypotenuse of a right triangle. You can ask the user either to input the triangle's largest side first or to input it last. What should the program do if the user does not comply with your request?

AVERAGING

Write a program which will compute the average of a list of numbers of unknown length. The program should also report the number of numbers in the list.

NOTES: Let the last entry be 999999 to indicate the end of the list. This value is not to be included in the average or the count. If there are N numbers in the list and these are

$$X_1, \ X_2, \ X_3, \ \ldots , \ X_N$$

then the average of these numbers is

$$Average \ = \frac{1}{N} \ (X_1 + X_2 + X_3 + \ldots + X_N)$$

Will your program work if there are no numbers in the list (the only entry being 999999)? This problem should be done without attempting to store the whole list in the computer's memory at one time.

INTEREST

If you put P dollars into a savings account with an interest rate R, compounded T times a year, how much money would be in the account at the end of N years? Write a program which will answer this question for any combination of the parameters P, R, T, and N. Then, use the program to determine the amount after one year, starting with $100 at 5 percent interest, when it is compounded (1) annually, (2) semiannually, (3) quarterly, and (4) daily.

NOTES: The amount A in the savings account is given by the formula

$$A = P \ [1 + (R/T)]^{NT}$$

where R is a decimal fraction, not a percent.

DIVIDING EVENLY

Write a program which will determine if one number is evenly divisible by another number. Your program should input the two numbers and print messages to give the results.

NOTES: There are at least three different ways to write such a program. If you have looked ahead in the book, the INT function must not be used.

TWO AT ONCE

Two linear equations may be represented by:

$$aX + bY = c$$
$$dX + eY = f$$

If these are to be solved simultaneously, their solution is the point at which they intersect, (X, Y) where:

$$X = \frac{ce - bf}{ae - bd}$$

$$Y = \frac{af - cd}{ae - bd}$$

Write a program which, when given the parameters a, b, c, d, e and f, will solve any two simultaneous linear equations for X and Y. Your program should allow for the possibility that ae = bd.

NOTES: You should be able to derive the formulas for X and Y shown above.

EQUATION OF A LINE

Write a program which will compute and print the equation of a straight line, $y = mx + b$, when given either (1) the slope m and one point, (x,y), on the line, or (2) two points, (x_1, y_1) and (x_2, y_2), on the line.

NOTES: You must allow for both cases within one program. The program may ask the user which case is to be computed.

Chapter 4
Loops

Many programs instruct a computer to repeat part of a program. For example, you could print the integers from 1 to 10 this way:

```
10 LET X=0
20 LET X=X+1
30 PRINT X
40 IF X<10 THEN 20
50 END
```

Since this kind of loop is common, computer languages simplify it. In BASIC, the first statement of a loop is expressed as shown in the box below.

```
# FOR variable = expression₁ TO ex-
  pression₂
```

This statement is followed by all the statements that are to be performed more than once. The last statement of the loop is then expressed as shown in the box below.

```
# NEXT variable
```

The FOR and NEXT statements can now be used to rewrite the counting program shown above:

```
10 FOR X=1 TO 10
20 PRINT X
30 NEXT X
40 END
```

The FOR statement here means the following: FOR all values of X (variable) from 1 (expression₁) to 10 (expression₂) in differences of 1, perform the statements between FOR and NEXT.

Note that the variable is automatically increased by 1 each time. This difference is called the "increment." The variable used in the FOR statement is called the "index."

What if we wanted to count from 1 to an unknown number N? This program will do it:

```
5 INPUT N
10 FOR X=1 TO N
```

```
20 PRINT X
30 NEXT X
40 END
```

Let's do another: Print all *even* integers from 1 to N. The FOR statement increases a variable by 1 each time. This problem, however, requires an increase of 2 each time. We could do it this way:

```
5 INPUT N
10 FOR X=1 TO N/2
20 PRINT 2*X
30 NEXT X
40 END
```

But again, there is a statement that makes it easier, as shown in the box.

```
# FOR variable = expn₁ TO expn₂
  STEP expn₃

  Do all statements between FOR and
  NEXT for each value of the variable
  starting with expression₁ through
  expression₂ increased by expression₃
  each time.
```

Thus, to print even integers, the easiest way is as follows:

```
5 INPUT N
10 FOR X=2 TO N STEP 2
20 PRINT X
30 NEXT X
40 END
```

You might want to use FOR/NEXT to rewrite the program which converted dollars to lira (Chap. 3). It can now be done with six statements.

Because of its use of an index and an increment, FOR/NEXT requires that you know how many times to repeat a loop, even if that is stated as an expression. Some loops must repeat indefinitely, however, until something happens to end them. In these cases, FOR/NEXT does *not* apply.

To illustrate indefinite loops, we will use some common programs. Every programmer learns from experience that certain routines are needed often. Having learned them, the programmer then has a bag of tricks which may be used over and over again. Several of these techniques appear below.

Adding

The problem is to sum the numbers in a sequence when (1) you do not know what the numbers are and (2) you do not know how many numbers there are (that is, the sequence is of unknown length). To solve the problem, we will need some number, not appearing in the sequence, to signal the end of the sequence. Let's choose this number, the last to be input, so that it is very large—say 999999. The flowchart appears in Fig. 4-1.

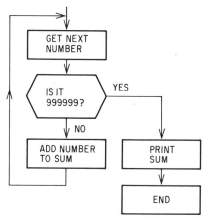

Fig. 4-1. Flowchart for adding

To write an adding program, we need one variable—say "X"—to hold each number in the sequence, one at a time. We need another variable—say "S"—to hold the sum. A variable used in this way is called an "accumulator." Then the adding program is:

```
10 LET S=0
20 INPUT X
30 IF X=999999 THEN 60
40 LET S=S+X
50 GOTO 20
60 PRINT "THE SUM IS "; S
70 END
```

Note that the number 999999 is not added to the sum.

Counting

The problem is to count a sequence of numbers of unknown length. That is, how many numbers are there in the sequence? Again, let 999999 represent

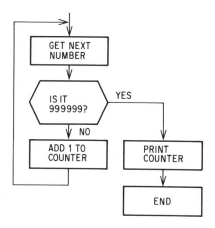

Fig. 4-2. Flowchart for counting

the end of the sequence. The counting procedure appears in Fig. 4-2.

Let variable X hold each number in the sequence, one at a time. Let variable N count how many numbers there are. A variable used in the latter way is called a "counter." The counting program is as follows:

```
10 LET N=0
20 INPUT X
30 IF X=999999 THEN 60
40 LET N=N+1
50 GOTO 20
60 PRINT "THERE ARE "; N; " NUMBERS."
70 END
```

Sorting

The problem is to sort a sequence of numbers in order of their size, the sequence being of unknown length. Since we are not yet ready to tackle this whole problem, let's try a smaller version of it: Sort any three numbers. We can "play computer" ourselves for this one. Suppose we drew four large boxes on a piece of paper, arranged as shown in Fig. 4-3. Then we could write any numbers—say 2, 3, and 4—on some cards and put them in the boxes. Suppose we put the 2 in A, the 4 in B, and the 3 in C.

If we want to sort the largest number first (in A), we must reverse the contents of A and B. Remember that the computer, with a LET statement, can move only one number at a time. Therefore, we must also move the cards one at a time. This is the purpose of box X. Put the 2 into X, then put the 4 into A, then put the 2 into B. (See Fig. 4-4.) A variable which is used as X is used here is called a "dummy variable."

The whole flowchart for sorting three numbers (regardless of how they are placed in A, B,

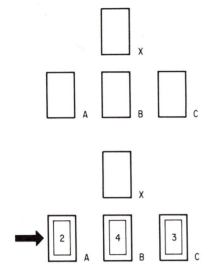

Fig. 4-3. Arrangement of boxes and numbers for sorting

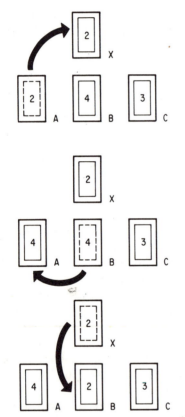

Fig. 4-4. Sorting for largest number first (beginning steps)

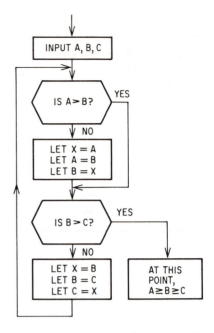

Fig. 4-5. Flowchart for sorting three numbers

Iteration

"Iteration" means estimating an answer by making closer and closer guesses. It is best explained by the flowchart shown in Fig. 4-6.

An example of iteration is finding square roots by averaging. Suppose you are given some number—say 6—and want to find its square root, $\sqrt{6}$. Guess a value for the square root—say 2. If this were the

and C) appears in Fig. 4-5. Try this procedure with the boxes and cards to see how it works. Then try writing a program which will follow the steps shown in the flowchart. (Sorting will again be discussed in Chap. 6.)

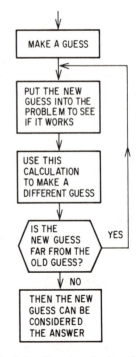

Fig. 4-6. Flowchart for iteration

correct value of the square root, and we divided the number by this value, the quotient would be equal to the guess. But when we divide 6 by 2, we get a quotient—3—which is larger than the guess. The square root is between 2 (too small) and 3 (too large). Therefore, average these—obtaining 2.5—and use this average as a new guess. Repeat the procedure, dividing and averaging again. This method is called "iterative" because it repeats and because each new guess will be closer to the actual square root.

Since the guesses will never be exactly equal to the square root of 6 (it is an irrational number), we need some way of deciding when to stop. Pick a very small number—say 0.00001—called the "degree of accuracy." When the difference between the guess and the quotient is less than this degree of accuracy, we are finished.

Here is a "desk check" of the whole calculation:

Guess = 2
   Quotient = 6/2 = 3
   Average = (2 + 3)/2 = 2.5
Guess = 2.5
   Quotient = 6/2.5 = 2.4
   Average = (2.5 + 2.4)/2 = 2.45
Guess = 2.45
   Quotient = 6/2.45 = 2.44898
   Average = (2.45 + 2.44898)/2 = 2.44949
Guess = 2.44949
   Quotient = 6/2.44949 = 2.44949
   Difference between quotient and guess is less than 0.00001; therefore the square root of 6 is 2.44949.

Problems

SQUARE ROOTS

Write a program which, when given any positive number, will find the square root of that number by using an averaging method.

NOTES: Print each guess used as the computer works through the problem. Let the first guess be 1. Let 0.00001 be the degree of accuracy. Will your program work for numbers less than 1?

SULTAN'S DILEMMA

An Arabian sultan called upon a neighboring chieftain to help him in a feud. The chief agreed and said that the price for his services would be all the grains of wheat placed on a checkerboard as follows: one grain on the first square, two grains on the second square, four grains on the third square, and so forth, doubling the number of grains each time. The sultan agreed and was driven into bankruptcy. How many grains were there?

If a bushel contains about 4.2×10^5 grains, how many bushels were there? Is this figure more or less than the yearly United States wheat crop of about 1.6×10^9 bushels?

NOTES: A checkerboard, of course, has 64 squares.

FACTORIALS

List, in two columns, the integers from 1 to 20 and their factorials.

NOTES: Given a number N, its factorial—written N! in mathematics—is:

$$N! = 1 * 2 * 3 * 4 * \ldots * (N-1) * N$$

Therefore:

$$
\begin{aligned}
1! &= 1 &&= 1 \\
2! &= 1 * 2 &&= 2 \\
3! &= 1 * 2 * 3 &&= 6 \\
4! &= 1 * 2 * 3 * 4 &&= 24
\end{aligned}
$$

And to be elegant:

$$N! = (N-1)! * N$$

FIBONACCI

Generate the Fibonacci sequence with a last term not to exceed 20,000. As you do this, also print the ratio between successive terms.

NOTES: The Fibonacci sequence is a string of numbers in which each successive number is formed by adding the two previous numbers. The sequence begins:

$$0 \quad 1 \quad 1 \quad 2 \quad 3 \quad 5 \quad 8 \quad \ldots .$$

What do you conclude about the ratio between terms?

DESCENDANTS

The United States Bicentennial was celebrated in 1976. Since a generation is considered to be twenty years, there were about ten generations between the Revolution and the Bicentennial. Consider what might have happened in ten generations. If a man and woman were married as colonists and had two children, and each of their children had two children, the sequence of offspring would be:

Generation:	1	2	3	...
Children:	2	4	8	...

Write a program which will print the whole sequence when each descendent has two children, when each descendent has three children, and when each descendent has four children. Print each sequence in a separate column.

NOTES: Although the numbers are theoretical, what conclusion do you draw? What factors other than birthrate would have influenced the size of the family tree over these 200 years?

FORTUNE TELLER

Write a program which will compute the amount of money accumulated in a savings bank account at the end of every year for a period of 20 years if the interest rate is 5 percent compounded daily and if the owner deposits $10 in the bank on the first day of every month.

NOTES: You may want to make your program more general, that is, for any number of years, for any rate of interest, and for any constant amount of regular monthly deposits.

WEIRD ROOT

Find the value of:

$$\sqrt{N + \sqrt{N + \sqrt{N + \sqrt{N + \ldots}}}}$$

for any positive integer N which may be input.

NOTES: How many square roots will you use? Although the problem shows a chain without end, we cannot let the computer run forever. Remember that

$$\sqrt{X} = X^{\frac{1}{2}}$$

COMPUTING PI

In 1673, a mathematician named Leibnitz showed that the value of one-fourth pi was equal to an infinitely long series:

$$\frac{\pi}{4} = 1 - \frac{1}{3} + \frac{1}{5} - \frac{1}{7} + \frac{1}{9} - \dots$$

Each fraction in this series is called a "term."

Use this series to compute the value of π correct to one decimal place. Your final solution should *not* print each term as it proceeds. How many terms of the series does the program use?

Now use the series to compute the value of π correct to two decimal places, and once again to three decimal places. Fill in this table:

Accuracy (decimal places)	Number of terms used
1	
2	
3	

Without doing the computation, how many terms would be needed for four-place accuracy? For six-place accuracy? Does this look like a good way to compute very exact values of π?

Chapter 5
Functions

To compute a common function, the square root of X, one could use either of the following statements:

```
# LET Y = X↑.5

# LET Y = X↑(1/2)
```

An easier way would be to use a "library" function provided by BASIC, as shown in the box below.

SQR(X)	square root of X, or $\sqrt{X}$

When given the value of X, SQR (X) returns the value of its square root. The variable X is called the "argument" of the function. An argument may be any expression. So to compute the hypotenuse of a right triangle, for instance, one could write:

```
# LET C = SQR(A↑2 + B↑2)
```

Computers differ in the kinds of functions they provide. The most common mathematical functions, in addition to SQR(X), are listed below. The argument of any function is an expression. A function may be used in any expression. The value of a function is computed first in the order of operations.

Mathematical functions

ABS(X)	Absolute value of X, or |X|
SGN(X)	Sign of X (+1 if X is positive; zero if X is zero; –1 if X is negative)
INT(X)	Largest integer contained in X

The function INT(X) returns the largest integer in X. For example, if X is 15.76, then INT(X) is 15. Or if X is –15.76, then INT(X) is –16. This function may be used to round off numbers. For instance,

1. To round to the nearest integer, use INT(X+.5).
2. To round to the nearest tenth, use INT(10*X+.5)/10.
3. To round to the nearest hundredth (two decimal places), use INT(100*X+.5)/100.

SIN(X)	Sine of angle of X radians
COS(X)	Cosine of angle of X radians
TAN(X)	Tangent of angle of X radians
ATN(X)	Arctangent of X (the angle in radians whose tangent is X)

Radians are a unit of measuring angles, like degrees. Given an angle measured in degrees, multiply it by $\pi/180$ to convert it to radians (π = 3.14159).

EXP(X)	e^X
LOG(X)	Natural logarithm of X, or $\log_e X$, or ln X

The log and exponent functions are "natural" functions that use base e (e = 2.71828). The "common" logarithm, using base 10, of X is equal to LOG(X)/LOG(10).

Random numbers

RND(X) or RND
Random number between 0 and 1 (independent of the value of X)

The function RND(X) returns a random number. This function is different from all others. Its value does not depend on its argument. Although the X in RND(X) is useless, it is necessary if the computer is to recognize RND as a function. Some computers allow the argument to be omitted.

As an example, we could generate five random numbers between 0 and 1 with this program:

```
10 FOR I=1 TO 5
20 PRINT RND(X)
30 NEXT I
40 END
```

On some large computers, this program may print a different set of random numbers each time it is run. But on most computers, it will print the same five numbers in every run. It is as if the computer had a list of "random" numbers and started at the same place in the list each time. To get different random numbers in each run, add a RANDOMIZE statement (see box) at the beginning of your program. It instructs the computer to start at a random place in its list of random numbers. That's really random!

RANDOMIZE

Start RND(X) with a different random number whenever a program is executed.

Table 5-1. The effects of a RANDOMIZE statement

```
                          5 RANDOMIZE
10 FOR I=1 TO 5           10 FOR I=1 TO 5
20 PRINT RND(X)           20 PRINT RND(X)
30 NEXT I                 30 NEXT I
40 END                    40 END

RUN                       RUN
 •204935                   •526361
 •229581                   •158092
 •533074                   •211307
 •132211                   •845011
 •995602                   •168303

READY                     READY

RUN                       RUN
 •204935                   •424366
 •229581                   •54614
 •533074                   •457542
 •132211                   •829992
 •995602                   •862078

READY                     READY
```

Using random numbers

If RND(X) produces a random number between 0 and 1, how could we obtain a random number between 0 and 2? That's easy. We would use the function 2*RND(X). And what if we wanted a random number between 3 and 5? That would be 2*(RND(X)+3. In general, a random number between A and B is given by (B − A)*RND(X) + A.

Suppose, however, that we are doing a coin tossing experiment. We need to generate a random *integer*—a 1 for heads and a 2 for tails. Remember that 2*RND(X) produces a random number between 0 and 2. By using INT(X), we can produce a random integer in this range. Thus, INT(2*RND(X)) will be either 0 or 1 at random. To do the coin tossing program, however, we will need INT(2*RND(X))+1, which will produce either 1 or 2 at random.

Do-it-yourself functions

If the library functions are not sufficient, you can build your own by using the DEF statement in the box.

DEF FNa(x) = expression

Define a function named FNa.

The DEF stands for "define." The name of your function must be composed of three letters, the first two of which must be FN. The expression may contain either one or two variables, and those must be the variables appearing as arguments of the function. For example, the following are legal:

```
# DEF FNM(K) = 3*SQR(K) - 2

# DEF FNA(X,Y) = X↑2 + Y↑2
```

But the following may not be used:

```
# DEF FNA(X) = X - Y

# DEF FNG(B) = 2*M + 5
```

The variables in a DEF statement are "dummy" variables, used only for defining the function. When the function is used in the program, any expression may appear as an argument. For example, suppose we want to find the distance D between two points, (X1,Y1) and (X2,Y2). The formula is:

$$D = \sqrt{(X2 - X1)^2 + (Y2 - Y1)^2}$$

One program to carry out this task might be the following:

Functions
37

```
10 DEF FND(C2,C1) = (C2 - C1)↑2        80 PRINT "DISTANCE IS "; D
20 PRINT "INPUT TWO POINTS"            90 END
30 INPUT X1,Y1
40 INPUT X2,Y2
50 LET A=FND(X2,X1)
60 LET B=FND(Y2,Y1)
70 LET D=SQR(A+B)
```

This program is for illustration and not the best way to do the task, but note that it is legal to use one pair of variables to define the function and a different pair when the function is called.

Problems

EUCLIDEAN ALGORITHM

Write a program which will find the greatest common factor (or greatest common denominator) of any two integers.

NOTES: A classic way to solve this problem is called the Euclidean Algorithm. Dividing any integer N by another integer D will produce a quotient, Q:

$$Q = INT(N/D)$$

and a remainder:

$$R = N - Q*D$$

The algorithm says first divide N by D and find R. If R is not zero, replace N by D and D by R, and divide again. Continue this process until R is zero. Then the last value of D is the Greatest Common Factor. For example, to find the GCF of 153 and 18, proceed as follows:

$$\frac{153}{18} = 8 + \frac{9}{18}$$

$$\frac{18}{9} = 2 + \frac{0}{9}$$

Thus, 9 is the greatest common factor.

DOLLARS AND POUNDS

Write a program which will convert any amount of American money into predecimal English currency at the rate of $1.75 to 1 pound.

NOTES: Predecimal English currency was:

> *1 pound = 20 shillings*
> *1 shilling = 12 pence*

Fractions of English pennies will not do. Great Britain, of course, no longer uses this system, having converted to decimal currency.

GUESS THE NUMBER (I)

Write a program which will pick a random integer between 1 and 99 (those values included) and then ask the user to guess what it is. For each try, it should tell whether the guess is too high or too low, until the user finally guesses the number. The program should write a congratulatory message if the user guesses the number in less than seven tries and a discouraging message if it takes more than seven tries.

EXECUTOR'S NIGHTMARE

A man, in his will, left instructions to his executor to distribute once a year a sum of exactly $660 among the poor of his parish. But the executor was only to continue the gift so long as he could distribute it in different ways, always giving $18 each to a certain number of children and $30 each to a certain number of adults.

Of course, by "different ways" is meant a different number of children and adults every time. During how many years could the charity be administered?

TEACHING ADDITION

Prepare a simple drill program for addition exercises. Print two random integers in a suitable format, for which the user must compute the sum. INPUT the user's answer and compare it with the correct answer. If the user's answer is not correct, repeat the same problem. If the user's answer is correct, print a message of encouragement and repeat the procedure with a new pair of numbers.

PRIMES

Write a program which will find all the prime numbers from 1 to 200.

NOTES: There are many methods which may be used, but a classic way to find all primes from 1 to some number N is the Sieve of Eratosthenes. It works as follows. Generate the list of integers from 1 to N. The integers 1 and 2 are known to be prime. Starting with 2, a prime, delete all multiples of 2 from the list. The next remaining number, which is 3, must be prime. Delete all multiples of 3 from the list. The next remaining number, which is 5, is prime. And so forth. At the end, all numbers not eliminated are prime. Obviously, this method takes many steps if the list is long. You may want to find a more efficient method.

QUADRATIC ROOTS

A quadratic equation has the form,

$$Ax^2 + Bx + C = 0$$

where A, B, and C are constant coefficients. The values of x which satisfy this equation are called "roots." There may be two roots for each equation, found by using the quadratic formula:

$$x_1 = \frac{-B + \sqrt{B^2 - 4AC}}{2A}$$

$$x_2 = \frac{-B - \sqrt{B^2 - 4AC}}{2A}$$

Write a program which will compute the roots of any quadratic equation, given the three coefficients.

NOTES: What if A is zero? What if $B^2 - 4AC$ is zero? What if $B^2 - 4AC$ is negative? Try using the following test data:

A	B	C
1	5	6
1	-1	6
1	0	-4
1	0	4
0	1	4
1	4	4
0	0	4
1	1	1
0	0	0

## Chapter 6

Subscripted Variables

In an earlier chapter, the computer's memory was compared to a set of pigeonhole mailboxes. Each place is named by a variable and can hold one number. So far, we have assumed that a variable can be any letter of the alphabet. This system would be awkward if we had more than 26 numbers to store. But often we find that lists of numbers are not values of different variables. They are just different values of one variable. These values can be stored at one time in a "list."

In mathematics, a list would be written:

$$x_1, x_2, x_3, x_4, \ldots , x_n$$

Each of these is a "subscripted variable" (the number is the subscript). They are read as "x sub one," "x sub two," and so forth. For the computer, this list would be written as follows:

$$X(1), X(2), X(3), X(4), \ldots , X(N)$$

Each of these is a variable and names a place in the memory which can hold one number. For instance, the value of X(3) could be 17. Each subscript indicates the position of a value in the list. For example, X(6) is the sixth item in a list called X. The variable N represents the list's largest subscript.

Where would one look for the fourth value of X? In X(4), of course. Remember that X(4) is the variable "x sub four," while X*4 is "x times four."

Subscripts must be integers. The largest possible subscript varies from computer to computer. The smallest subscript may be either zero or one, depending on the machine you are using. It is a good idea to form the habit of *not* using zero. The computer's memory, for any one variable, then looks something like Fig. 6-1.

There is one other hitch to writing a program which uses a list. We must include a DIM (for DIMENSION) statement to set aside space in the memory for each list to be used.

DIM variable(m), variable(n), . . .

Reserve space for lists.

Fig. 6-1. Memory for numeric variable X (partial)

Suppose we want the subscripts 1 to 99 for X(I). Before using X(I), there must appear in the program the statement,

```
# DIM X(99)
```

Some computers may reserve up to ten spaces for each list automatically. But always using DIM is a good habit, especially since a program need not use all the reserved places.

Note that X(N) and X(I) have been used to represent a list. The subscript can itself be an ordinary variable or any expression. If the expression happens not to have an integer value, it will automatically be rounded off by most computers.

As examples of lists, we will consider some common procedures.

Storing

Frequently, programmers need to store in the computer's memory a list of numbers of unknown length. To do this, we will designate a list—say A(N)—and, as we have done before, we will let the last number in the sequence be 999999. The variable N represents the position of each number.

The flowchart shown in Fig. 6-2 produces this program:

```
10 DIM A(999)
20 LET N=0
30 LET N=N+1
40 INPUT A(N)
50 IF A(N)<>999999 THEN 30
60 END
```

46

Fig. 6-2. Storing

This program simply stores numbers in the memory. When the program reaches line 60, the list is stored in:

$$A(1), \ A(2), \ A(3), \ \ldots, \ A(N-1)$$

and the number 999999 is stored in A(N), whatever N might be. Not counting 999999, how many numbers are there in the list? There are N-1 numbers. So N, in this example, is both a changeable subscript and a counter.

If, after storing the numbers, we wanted to use them, then we would extend the program starting at line 60. For example:

are switched. This process is repeated until no more exchanges are needed.

2. SELECTION: The smallest (or largest) item is found and placed first in the sorted list. Then the next smallest (or largest) item is found. This process is repeated until all items have been placed.

3. DISTRIBUTION: A counter is assigned to each item which may appear. The items in the list are then considered one at a time. As each item occurs, the appropriate counter is incremented. Finally, all items may be printed, the number of times being determined by the counters.

Other schemes for sorting include insertion, enumeration, and radix methods.

The procedure for sorting three numbers (Chap. 4) is an example of an exchange sort. To sort more than three numbers, a similar program may be designed. A flowchart for this program appears in Fig. 6-3. An exchange sort, however, is very inefficient for long lists.

The flowchart in Fig. 6-3 is known as a "bubble sort" because a number that starts at the wrong end of the list will move up (or down) one position with each pass through the program. The program will run until it makes a complete pass through the list with no exchanges. The list is then in order.

```
10  DIM A(999)
20  LET N=0
30  LET N=N+1
40  INPUT A(N)
50  IF A(N)<>999999 THEN 30
60  REM *** INPUT LOOP ENDS.
70  PRINT "THERE ARE "; N-1; " NUMBERS"
80  PRINT "IN THIS LIST.  THEY ARE:"
90  REM *** OUTPUT LOOP BEGINS.
100 FOR K=1 TO N-1
110 PRINT A(K)
120 NEXT K
130 END
```

This program uses one subscript, N, to store and a different subscript, K, to print the list. Since N holds the count of entries in the list, we don't want to change it by using it as the index in the FOR/ NEXT output loop.

Sorting

There are many ways to sort lists. Three simple algorithms are:

1. EXCHANGE: Items are considered two at a time. If they are out of order, their positions

In Fig. 6-3, the step "GET LIST X(K)" represents a storing program like that shown earlier in this chapter. The variable K is an index, and the variable C counts the exchanges made in one pass through the list. This sort will work if there are at least two items in the list. The sorted list will be in order of decreasing size:

$$X(1) > X(2) > X(3) > \ldots > X(N-1)$$

It should not be forgotten that X(N) has the value 999999.

Subscripted Variables

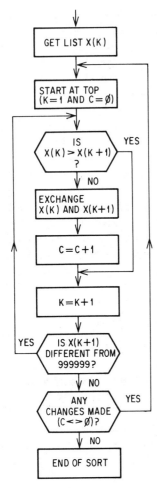

Fig. 6-3. Exchange or "bubble" sort

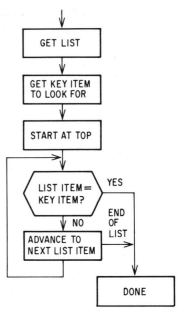

Fig. 6-4. Searching

Searching

Suppose we are given a list of numbers of unknown length. We would like to know how many times a number Y appears, and at which positions in the list. This search will have one of two results, either "item found" (with positions) or "item not found."

The easiest way to do this is by a "sequential search." Just look through the whole list, one item at a time, until the item is found or until the end of the list appears (see Fig. 6-4). Note that the item we are looking for may appear more than once.

If the list happens to be sorted in increasing order, we do not have to search to the end of the list. We can quit when an item in the list is larger than the item we are looking for.

This sequential search is not good to use on long lists. There are other ways to search, including the "binary search" used in playing "Guess The Number" (see problems in previous chapter).

Tables

On most computers, double subscripts are also available. A variable with a single subscript is called a "list." For example, A(7) is the seventh item in a list named A. A variable with a double subscript is called a "table." For example, D(3,5) is the item in the third row and fifth column of a table named D.

A list may also be called a "vector," and a table may also be called a "matrix." Either may be called an "array." For any variable, therefore, the computer's memory looks a bit like Fig. 6-5.

In one program, both an ordinary variable—like X—and a subscripted variable with the same letter—like X(I) or X(J,K)—may be used. But a list—like X(I)—and a table—like X(J,K)—for the same variable may not be used in the same program.

The operations of adding, counting, and searching may be performed on tables as well as lists. For example, suppose we want to sum all the items in a table, E(I,J), if R is the number of items in each row and C is the number of items in each column. Then, across each row, we have to add all the column entries, as follows:

```
20 FOR J=1 TO C
30 LET S = S + E(I,J)
40 NEXT J
```

and we have to do this for all the rows, as follows:

```
10 FOR I=1 TO R
20 FOR J=1 TO C
30 LET S = S + E(I,J)
```

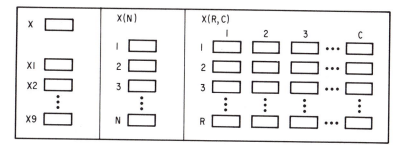

Fig. 6-5. Memory for numeric variable X

```
40 NEXT J
50 NEXT I
```

Putting one loop inside another is called "nesting." The nested (inside) loop must be entirely contained within the outer loop.

```
┌──►10 FOR I=1 TO R
│ ┌►20 FOR J=1 TO C
│ │  30 LET S = S + E(I,J)
│ └─40 NEXT J
└───50 NEXT I
```

A program like this would be useful for keeping track of a weekly budget. The rows could represent the days of the week (from 1 to 7) and the columns might represent the type of expense:

1. Rent and utilities
2. Groceries
3. Transportation
4. Clothing and entertainment
5. Medical fees and insurance
6. Savings

To sum the expenses for a week, one could adopt the following program:

```
10 DIM E(7,6)
20 LET S=0
30 REM *** I=DAYS, J=CATEGORIES
40 FOR I=1 TO 7
50    FOR J=1 TO 6
60       PRINT "INPUT: DAY "; I; " CATEGORY "; J
70       INPUT E(I,J)
80       LET S = S + E(I,J)
90    NEXT J
100 NEXT I
110 PRINT "TOTAL IS $"; S
120 END
```

Problems

PYTHAGOREAN TRIPLES

Find all sets of positive integers X, Y, and Z, each less than 20, that satisfy the equation,

$$X^2 + Y^2 + Z^2 = N^2$$

where N is also an integer.

COUNTING VOTES

It is possible to write a program which will count the votes in an election, or tabulate the responses to a questionnaire, or tally any other list of numbers. The input data for such a program might be a sequence of one-digit numbers, where "4" would represent one vote for candidate Number 4.

Write a program which, when given any list of one-digit numbers, will tell how many 1's there are in the list, how many 2's, and so forth. When the program reaches the end of the list, it should also print the total number of numbers tallied. Don't forget that zero is a digit.

TALLYING AGAIN

Write a program which will tally the digits in a sequence of four-digit numbers. Tabulate each position separately. For example, if the numbers given were 103, 569, 624, and 961, then the result would be:

TALLY	THOU'S	HUND'S	TENS	UNITS
ZERO	0	0	1	0
ONE	0	1	0	1
TWO	0	0	1	0
THREE	0	0	0	1
.	.	.	.	.
.	.	.	.	.
.	.	.	.	.
NINE	0	1	0	1

NOTES: See the previous problem, "Counting Votes," for hints.

SEARCHING

Write a program which will generate and store a list of 999 random integers between 1 and 999, will ask the user what number to search for, and will then print the number of times that that number appears in the list.

NOTES: In order to search easily, the list should be sorted. An exchange sorter will not handle a list this long (it would require about a million passes through the list!). However, sorting by distribution can be used. Establish a counter, C(X), for each possible random integer X. Then every time an integer is produced by the random-number generator, increment its counter by 1. What will your program do if the number you are searching for is not in the list? It is very unlikely that every integer between 1 and 999 will be in the list.

REARRANGEMENT

Given any mixed-up sequence of numbers, write a program which will print them in order of increasing size (smallest first). Use an exchange sorter.

NOTES: Here are two lists to be used for testing your program:

LIST A	LIST B
4640	9856
6088	4911
2081	5761
4770	8917
9847	4912
4473	5761
7989	2207
5353	2274
4261	7728
6195	5761

Will your program work if the list is empty (the only entry being 999999)? What if the list contains just one item?

MERGING

Suppose we are given two lists, each sorted in order of increasing (or decreasing) size. "Merging" would combine them so that they formed a single list, also properly sorted in order of size. The starting lists do not have to be the same length. Write a program which will merge two lists of numbers and print the result.

NOTES: Typical lists may be obtained from the output of the "Rearrangement" problem.

DECIMAL TO BINARY

Write a program which, when given any decimal number, will change that number to base 2 and print the binary result.

NOTES: A change from base 10 to base 2 is shown in this example:

$$41 = 32 + 8 + 1$$
$$41 = (1 \times 2^5) + (0 \times 2^4) + (1 \times 2^3) + (0 \times 2^2) + (0 \times 2^1) + (1 \times 2^0)$$

Decimal   41 = 101001   Binary

THREE AT ONCE

Write a program which will solve any three simultaneous linear equations.

NOTES: Refer to the earlier problem with two equations for hints. Ask your teacher to explain Cramer's Rule.

GAMBLER'S PAYOFF

Seven men sat at a gambling table and agreed that whenever a player lost a game, he would double the money of each of the other players—that is, he was to give the other players each as much money as they then had in their pockets.

They played seven games and each lost a game in turn. Oddly, when they had finished, each man had exactly the same amount—$32—in his pocket.

How much money did each man have before he sat down to play?

Chapter 7
More About Input/Output

So far, we have discussed two ways that a computer can assign a value to a variable. It can compute the number in a LET statement. Or it can get the number from the keyboard via an IN-PUT statement.

Because it is time-consuming, INPUT may sometimes be unsatisfactory. The computer must halt and wait for the programmer to provide information. Other times, the computer may need a "library" of numbers or words to use as a reference.

On such occasions, one would use a READ statement and a DATA statement. Where INPUT means "get a value from the keyboard," READ means "get a value from a DATA statement."

```
# READ variable, variable, . . .

    Get values of variables from DATA
```

```
# DATA constant, constant, . . .

    Values for variables in READ.
```

A DATA statement is ignored when the computer executes statements in numerical order. If more than one item is listed in a DATA statement, READ will take them in order until there is no more data. For example,

```
10 READ X,Y
20 PRINT X,Y
30 GOTO 10
40 DATA 1, 2, 3, 4, 5, 6
50 END

RUN
 1               2
 3               4
 5               6
OUT OF DATA AT LINE 10

READY
```

The "out of data" line printed by the computer could be eliminated by a FOR/NEXT loop:

```
5 FOR N=1 TO 3
10 READ X,Y
20 PRINT X,Y
30 NEXT N
40 DATA 1, 2, 3, 4, 5, 6
50 END
```

A DATA statement may be placed anywhere in the program before END. But you should adopt the habit of placing DATA statements at the end (or at the beginning) of a program. DATA statements scattered throughout a program are usually confusing. To use a DATA list over again in the same program, insert RESTORE.

```
# RESTORE

    Allow READ to start at beginning
    of DATA.
```

For example:

```
5 FOR N=1 TO 3
10 READ X,Y
20 PRINT X,Y
30 NEXT N
40 RESTORE
50 GOTO 5
60 DATA 1, 2, 3, 4, 5, 6
70 END

RUN
 1               2
 3               4
 5               6
 1               2
 3               4
 5               6
 1               2
 3               4
```

How can this program be stopped? On some computers, pressing CTRL/C (the CTRL or "control" key and the C key simultaneously) will halt a program that is being executed. On other computers, the BREAK or BRK key is used for this purpose. All computers have some sort of a "panic button."

To have this program run through the DATA list three times and then stop without CTRL/C or BREAK, one would use a "nested" loop (a loop within a loop):

```
 4 FOR C=1 TO 3
 5 FOR N=1 TO 3
10 READ X,Y
20 PRINT X,Y
30 NEXT N
40 RESTORE
50 NEXT C
60 DATA 1, 2, 3, 4, 5, 6
70 END
```

Controlling output format

The function TAB(X) instructs the computer to move the typing head of the terminal to space X. On some computers, the function may be changed slightly, so that the head moves to space X+1, thus bypassing X spaces. To find out how your computer operates, try running a program like that at the top of the right-hand column.

```
10 FOR X=0 TO 5
20 PRINT TAB(X); "***"
30 NEXT X
40 END

RUN
***
  ***
    ***
      ***
        ***
          ***

READY
```

The argument of TAB(X) can be any expression. If the value of the expression happens not to be an integer, most computers will automatically round it off. However, programmers often insure the argument's being an integer by using INT(X) in their programs. TAB(X) will obviously not work if the argument is negative.

TAB(X) is very useful. For example, the computer can plot a mathematical function, as shown at the bottom of this page.

*[handwritten: FOR Y=30 TO 0 / PRINT TAB(Y); "***"]*

```
10 FOR X=0 TO 10
20 LET Y = X↑2-4
30 IF Y<0 THEN 70
40 IF Y>50 THEN 70
50 PRINT TAB(Y); "*"
60 GOTO 80
70 PRINT
80 NEXT X
90 END

RUN


     *
        *
           *
              *
                 *
                    *

READY
```

As the computer prints the graph, values of Y appear horizontally across the page and values of X appear vertically down the page. To be seen normally, the paper must be given a one-quarter turn counterclockwise. (Plotting is discussed in Chap. 9.)

Trailing semicolons and commas

A typical INPUT statement might look like this:

```
.
.
30 PRINT "HOW MANY NUMBERS"
40 INPUT M
.
.
RUN

HOW MANY NUMBERS
?
```

It would be more elegant if the question mark appeared at the exact end of the message, rather than on the next line. This will do it:

```
.
.
30 PRINT "HOW MANY NUMBERS";
40 INPUT M
.
.
RUN

HOW MANY NUMBERS?
```

The trailing semicolon (line 30) says to the computer, "Keep printing on the same line; more follows." The trailing semicolon can only be used in a PRINT statement. It often saves paper, as shown in the run at the bottom of this page.

A trailing comma works the same as a trailing semicolon, but as would be expected, spaces the output in columns.

An aside: games as problems for computer solution

All games have rules. These specify the playing field, the order of play, the scoring, and the situation which ends the game. Some games also involve "strategy." Strategy is never printed in a rule book. It determines each player's conduct during the game. Strategy can be a series of IF-THEN statements which tell a player how to win the game, depending on what the other players do. Different players may have different strategies for playing the same game.

When computers are programmed to play games, they don't win because they are smarter than human beings. They win when the human being who programs them discovers a winning strategy. "One Pile" (also known as "Twenty-three Matches" or "Battle of Numbers") is a good example of this. The rules are simple: A number of objects—say 23—are placed in a pile. Two players alternately draw from the pile. Each player may take 1, 2, or 3 objects on a draw. Neither player may skip a turn. The player who takes the last object wins.

To derive the winning strategy, consider what happens at the end of a game. If a player finds just four objects left in the pile, he has lost. Whatever he takes, his opponent can take the remainder and win. In order to leave four objects, the other player must have left eight objects on the turn just before. The number he has left in the pile on any of his turns, in fact, has been a multiple of four. And four happens to be the sum of the smallest and largest possible draws.

Thus, the winning strategy is, "If possible, remove just enough objects to leave (S + L)*N objects in the pile," where S is the smallest number that can be drawn, L is the largest number that can be drawn, and N is an integer (depending on what turn it is). If the number of objects in the original pile is (S + L)*N, the first player should lose. If it is not, the first player can win by always reducing the pile to (S + L)*N.

```
10 FOR X=1 TO 10
20 PRINT " "; X;
30 NEXT X
40 END

RUN
    1    2    3    4    5    6    7    8    9    10
READY
```

If you do not believe this strategy, try it with a friend. Also try changing the rules so that up to four objects can be drawn on a turn. Does the formula still work? Try changing the rules again so that the player who takes the last object loses. Can you find a winning strategy for this situation?

Problems

POPULATION DENSITY

The first United States census included seventeen states with a total land area of about 433,000 square miles. Over the next 180 years, the population of these states increased steadily:

Year	Population (millions)
1790	3.9
1800	5.2
1810	6.8
1820	8.4
1830	10.5
1840	12.2
1850	15.1
1860	18.0
1870	20.0
1880	24.2
1890	28.5
1900	33.9
1910	40.2
1920	45.5
1930	51.8
1940	55.1
1950	61.3
1960	69.7
1970	77.6

Write a program which, given only the actual populations in DATA statements, will print in three columns: the years (as shown above), the population (as shown above), and the average number of people per square mile (to the nearest integer).

GEOMETRIC SERIES

A geometric series is a sum in which any two successive terms have a common ratio. A geometric series with 20 terms and a common ration R would be:

$$SUM = 1 + R + R^2 + R^3 + R^4 + \ldots + R^{18} + R^{19}$$

Write a program which will compute the sum of 20 terms of a geometric series, printing the sum as it accumulates term-by-term. Do this for the following values of R: 1/4, 1/2, 3/4, 1, and 2. Print the results in a table as follows:

	VALUE OF R				
Terms	0.25	0.5	0.75	1	2
1	1	1	1	1	1
2					
3					
...		and so forth			
19					
20					

Note that when R is zero, the sum is one, no matter how many terms there are. What conclusion do you draw from this experiment?

GUESS THE NUMBER (II)

Having written the program which picks a random integer and asks the user to guess what it is, write a program which does the reverse. The user will pick a number between 1 and 99, and the computer has to guess it in less than seven tries.

NOTES: In order to write such a program, you have to figure out the difference between a good sequence of guesses and a bad sequence. The good sequence may be called a "binary search." "Guess the Number" is a game of skill, not a game of strategy. The player should be able to "win" every time by using seven or fewer guesses, provided he discovers the skill. In this game, the skill is a mathematical trick which may be discovered by playing "Guess the Number I" a few times.

CHANGEMAKER

Write a program which will act as an automatic changemaker. When given the amount of a bill and the amount of money to be paid, it should print both the total amount of change to be returned and the denominations to be used (as few pieces of paper currency or coins as possible). Use the following denominations only:

Currency — TWENTIES, TENS, FIVES, ONES
Coins — QUARTERS, DIMES, NICKELS, PENNIES

FACTORING

Write a program which will find the prime factors of any given integer.

NOTES: You may have to impose a limit on how large the integer in question may be. Note that a factor may be used more than once in any given integer, for example:

$$100 = 2 \ x \ 2 \ x \ 5 \ x \ 5$$

What will your program do if the given integer is prime? You may want to ask your teacher or librarian for help in finding out about Fermat's method.

ONE PILE

Write a program which will play the game of One Pile. Can a program be written to let either the computer or the user move first? What should the program do if the user moves first and reduces the pile to (S + L)*N? How could a user cheat at this game? Could a program detect it?

PAYROLL

Write a program to compute the weekly payroll for a company with nine employees.

Regular wages are paid for 40 hours per week. Overtime is paid at time-and-a-half. Deductions include Federal income tax, state income tax, and FICA (Social Security) tax.

Federal income tax is T percent of gross pay:

$$T = INT(.0425*P + 14)$$

where T is a percent and P is weekly gross pay in dollars.

State income tax is 6 percent of gross pay.

FICA is 4.8 percent of gross pay up to $150 per week. If gross pay is over $150 per week, then the maximum FICA tax is 4.8 percent of $150.

For example, someone earning $200 per week would pay:

$$T = INT(.0425*200 + 14) = 22\%$$

or $44 in Federal income tax. He would also pay $12 in State income tax and the maximum FICA tax of $7.20. These deductions would leave him $136.80 in net pay to take home.

The output of your program should have the following format:

EMP	HRS	RATE	GROSS PAY	FED TAX	ST TAX	FICA	NET PAY
1	32	4.25					
2	40	3.50					
3	48	3.00					
4	48	3.00					
5	42	4.10					
6	50	4.00					
7	35	6.60					
8	52	5.25					
9	40	7.85					

What aspects of your program lead you to think that the BASIC we have learned so far is not adequate for doing business problems simply?

Chapter 8
Strings

A letter, say X, names a "numeric" variable, so-called because its value is a number. A letter in combination with a dollar sign, say X\$, names an "alphanumeric" variable. This kind of variable can store a message. Messages may include letters, punctuation marks, or spaces. Each letter, digit, or space is called a "character." Any sequence of characters is called a "string." So the value of an alphanumeric variable is a string.

String variables have a lot in common with numeric variables. They may be loaded via INPUT statements, as follows:

```
10  INPUT A$
20  INPUT B$
30  PRINT A$;B$
40  END

RUN
?  HELLO
?  THERE!
HELLO THERE!

READY
```

String variables may also be used in PRINT, READ, LET, and IF-THEN statements. However, strings which appear literally in a program must be enclosed in quotation marks:

```
10  READ A$,B$
20  PRINT A$;B$
30  DATA "55 ", "MPH"
40  END

10  LET A$="EGAD!"
20  LET B$=A$
30  PRINT B$
40  END

10  PRINT RND(0)
20  PRINT "ANOTHER";
30  INPUT A$
```

```
40  IF A$="YES" THEN 10
50  END
```

In IF-THEN statements, relations refer to sequence, as in it is true that "A"<"B". Obviously, words can be sorted in alphabetic order, just as we have already sorted numbers. Some computers, by the way, also provide string functions.

So far, so good. But how many characters may be assigned to each string variable? Computers differ. Several arrangements are described in the sections which follow. Only one of these sections will apply to any given computer.

Fixed length variables: less than a line

Some computers provide enough space in each string variable for a certain number of characters. This number may be from 6 to 22 characters, depending on the machine. Thus the longest string which may be stored in a variable is less than a line of terminal printing. The "length" of these string variables cannot be modified.

Consider a computer which reserves space in each variable for six characters. If fewer than six are stored, the remaining spaces will be filled with blanks. If more than six are provided, the excess will be ignored:

```
10  READ X$
20  PRINT X$
30  DATA "JUST SIX"
40  END

RUN
JUST S

READY
```

In this case, subscripts for string variables are exactly like subscripts for numeric variables. For instance, A\$(1) and A\$(2) are two variable places, each capable of holding one six-character string. The DIM statement tells the computer how many places to reserve. For instance, # DIM X$(9) reserves nine places for the list X$(N), each place being six characters long.

To input a string longer than six characters, a special form of INPUT may be available, called LINPUT.

```
# LINPUT variable

    Input long string.
```

LINPUT puts the first six characters into the location with subscript 1, the next six into the place with subscript 2, and so forth. For example,

```
10 DIM A$(4)
20 LINPUT A$
30 FOR N=1 TO 3
40 PRINT A$(N)
50 NEXT N
60 END

RUN
?THIS IS A MESSAGE.
THIS I
S A ME
SSAGE.

READY
```

Fixed length variables: a line or longer

Some computers reserve enough space in each string variable for a large number of characters. This number may be from 64 or 72 to thousands of characters, depending on the machine. The longest string which may be stored in a variable is thus as long as a line of terminal printing, or longer. However, the "length" of each string variable cannot be modified.

In such computers, subscripts for string variables are exactly like subscripts for numeric variables. For example, B$(1) and B$(2) are two variables, each capable of holding one string. The DIM statement tells the computer how many places to reserve. (The length of strings allowed in arrays may be shorter than the length of ordinary string variables.)

Except for string length, this arrangement looks like that described in the previous section. There is another difference, however. In this case, the LINPUT statement has a new meaning. Each

time a string value is required, LINPUT now assigns an entire line to the appropriate variable. A "line" consists of all characters typed before pressing the RETURN key. If more than one variable is listed, more than one line will be requested. This feature lets you input characters that might otherwise have a special meaning (for example, commas may be included in a LINPUT string).

```
# LINPUT variable, variable, . . .
    or
# INPUT LINE variable

    Assign entire line of input to each
    variable.
```

Declared length variables

Some computers allow the number of character spaces in each string to vary. The programmer must say how many there will be in each variable, up to a certain maximum dictated by the machine.

DIM tells such a computer how long each string variable will be. The statement # DIM X$(9) reserves space for nine characters in the variable X$. If fewer than the dimensioned number are provided, the remaining spaces will be filled with blanks. If more than the dimensioned number are provided, an error will result.

Subscripts have a different meaning here. A single subscript denotes that portion of the string beginning at the subscript position and continuing to the end of the variable. For example, suppose we have dimensioned X$ with four spaces and stored the letters A, B, C, and D in X$. Then X$(3) refers to CD.

Position	1	2	3	4
Value of X$	A	B	C	D

A double subscript denotes that portion of the string beginning with the first subscript position and ending with the second subscript position. In the above example, X$(2,3) refers to BC.

Single subscripts must start at one. In double subscripts, the second must be equal to or larger than the first subscript. As an example, see the program at the top of the next page.

```
10 DIM X$(6)
20 DATA "ABCDEF"
30 READ X$
40 FOR K=1 TO 6
50 PRINT K, X$(K), X$(K,K), X$(K,K+1)
60 NEXT K
70 END

RUN
1          ABCDEF        A           AB
2          BCDEF         B           BC
3          CDEF          C           CD
4          DEF           D           DE
5          EF            E           EF
6          F             F           F

READY
```

Problems

SORTING WORDS

Given any sequence of mixed-up words, write a program which will print them in alphabetic order.

BINARY ADDITION

Binary numbers can be added digit by digit, just like decimal numbers, from right to left. Write a program which will add any two binary numbers, each up to nine bits long, and print the sum in binary.

NOTES: The rules for adding binary digits are:

$$0 + 0 = 0$$
$$0 + 1 = 1$$
$$1 + 0 = 1$$
$$1 + 1 = 0 \ and \ carry \ 1$$
$$1 + 1 + 1 = 1 \ and \ carry \ 1$$

MAKING WORDS

From six vowels (AEIOUY) and the six most common consonants (DHNRST), the following number of three-letter words may be formed:

Three consonants	120
Two consonants, one vowel	540
One consonant, two vowels	540
Three vowels	120
Total	1320

What are the three-letter "words" with two consonants and one vowel? How many of them are real words?

NOTES: Print at least ten words on every line of output. Some corporations look for trademarks and product names by generating "words" the same way this exercise does.

CHECKWRITER

When writing a check, the amount must be shown twice, as both words and numbers. If you worked for a company where the payroll was figured on a computer (as in an earlier problem), the last step in that procedure would be for the machine to print the paychecks.

Write a program to print checks in amounts up to $999.99. The program should read each employee's name and net wages from DATA statements.

NOTES: An example of one such check might be:

> *******PAY TO THE ORDER OF: JOHN DOE. $267.98*
> *EXACTLY TWO HUNDRED SIXTY-SEVEN AND 98/100 DOLLARS*****

In this example, the values of string variables are the employee's name and the words "TWO," "HUNDRED," "SIXTY," and "SEVEN." You will need to store the following words in string variables:

Words needed	Word strings	Total characters
NO	*1*	*2*
ONE TO NINE	*9*	*36*
TEN TO NINETEEN	*10*	*70*
TWENTY TO NINETY	*8*	*47*
HUNDRED	*1*	*7*

SIMILES

A simile, for the purposes of this problem, is a four-word phrase:

(Adjective) AS A (Noun)

For example, TALL AS A TREE or STRONG AS A BULL.
  Write a program which will generate random similes.

NOTES: You will have to provide a dictionary of adjectives and nouns in DATA statements. What is the difference between a simile and a metaphor?

SENTENCE WRITER

Write a program which will generate random four-word sentences from a dictionary of nouns, verbs, adjectives, and adverbs, as follows: THE (adjective) (noun) (verb) (adverb).

RIGHT JUSTIFICATION

Write a program which will read a paragraph of text (either from DATA or INPUT) and will reprint it in the middle 50 spaces of a page. The right and left margins of the printout must be straight lines, and the last word in each line must be complete.

NOTES: This goal can be achieved by inserting extra blanks between words so that the length of each line is exactly 50 characters (neither beginning nor ending with a blank).

MORSE CODE

Write a program which will translate an alphabetic message into Morse code.

NOTES: After finishing this program, you may want to write a program which does the opposite.

ROMAN NUMERALS

Write a program which, given any Arabic numeral, will print its Roman numeral equivalent.

NOTES: The Roman numeral system is:

I	*1*	*C*	*100*
V	*5*	*D*	*500*
X	*10*	*M*	*1000*
L	*50*	*V*	*5000*

Repeating a letter repeats its value. This is done for numbers up to one less than the next new numeral. Examples:

II = 2	*XX = 20*
III = 3	*XXX = 30*

A letter placed before one of greater value subtracts therefrom. This is done only for the number which is one place less than the next new numeral. Examples:

IV = 4	*XL = 40*
IX = 9	*XC = 90*

A letter placed after one of greater value adds thereto. This is done for numbers following each new numeral. Examples:

VI = 6	*LX = 60*

Note especially that Roman numerals comprise a base 5 system.

## Chapter 9

Developing Larger Programs

The longer a program is, the harder it is to write because it is difficult to keep track of what must be done. Developing programs becomes easier, however, if you don't try to do the whole job all at once. Do it one step at a time. At each stage, refine your understanding of the problem, and make your solution more precise.

HOW TO WRITE A PROGRAM

1. Begin with a statement of the job and a rough idea of how to do it.
2. Identify output and input.
3. Break up the job into tasks, stated in your own words, in the order in which they must be done.
4. Identify variables to be used.
5. Program each task and assemble the pieces.
6. Test the program, and fix it if necessary.

This chapter shows how to implement the method outlined above. Plotting has been chosen as an example, because displaying results in graphic form is an important part of many programs. Later, subroutines will be introduced to show how pieces of a program can be written separately.

Plotting: Step 1

Our goal is simple. We want the computer to plot the graph of a continuous function in the first quadrant. This will be Y as a function of X. There are several ways to plot graphs at the terminal. A program shown earlier (Chap. 7) contained the TAB function:

```
10 FOR X=0 TO 10
20 LET Y = X↑2-4
30 IF Y<0 THEN 70
40 IF Y>50 THEN 70
50 PRINT TAB(Y); "*"
60 GOTO 80
```

```
70 PRINT
80 NEXT X
90 END
```

Using TAB is the basic *idea* we will adopt to solve the problem. Remember that as the computer prints the graph, values of X will appear vertically down the page, and values of Y will appear horizontally across the page. Also, the argument of TAB must be greater than or equal to zero, and less than the number of spaces in a line of terminal printing.

Plotting: Step 2

A sketch of the desired output is shown in Fig. 9-1. The input should consist of the largest value of X and the X increment (the distance between values of X). The function to be plotted will be built into the program. It should appear first, however, so that it can be changed easily.

Plotting: Step 3

What tasks must be done to produce the output of Fig. 9-1? To begin with, a program must:
1. Define the function to be plotted
2. Ask for the largest value of X and the X increment
3. Shrink the scale of Y to fit evenly on the page
4. Print the Y axis
5. On each line thereafter, print an X-axis mark and/or a point on the graph.

Why would we want to shrink the scale of Y? The Y axis is 50 spaces long. Values of Y greater than 50 will cause the graph to run off the page. The graph will fit only if each space across the page represents several Y units.

To shrink the scale of Y, the program must compute a "scale factor." Because the whole graph is 50 spaces wide, the scale factor will be 50 divided by the largest value of Y to be plotted. For example, the scale factor is 0.25 when the largest value of Y is 200. Each space across the page will represent four units of Y. When plotting

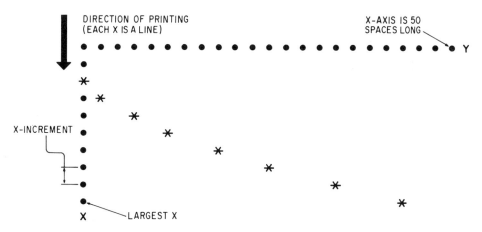

Fig. 9-1. Sketch of desired plotter output

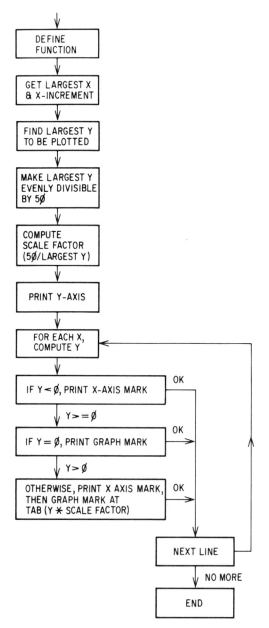

Fig. 9-2. Tasks for "1st Quadrant Plot"

each point, the value of Y times the scale factor equals the correct number of spaces across the page.

The flowchart in Fig. 9-2 shows all the tasks which must be done. Note that when the graph is actually printed, there are three choices. If Y is less than zero, only an X-axis mark is printed. If Y is equal to zero, only a graph mark is printed. If Y is greater than zero, both marks are printed, using TAB and the scale factor.

Plotting: Step 4

Let B represent the largest value of X, and let C be the X increment. Let M be the largest value of Y, and let K be the scale factor.

Plotting: Steps 5 and 6

The complete plotting program appears on the next page. REM statements have been included where appropriate.

Since this program meets the goal we set in the beginning (as shown by executing the RUN), we are done. More information about plotters can be found in the Appendix.

This step-by-step method is used by the best of programmers. When working on complicated jobs, they apply it over and over again. You may want to review the steps listed at the beginning of the chapter. Being orderly and disciplined will enable you to solve some very tough problems.

Subroutines

A subroutine is a "program within a program," that is, a sequence of statements to perform a given task. Subroutines make it easier to develop large programs. If a task is to be done several times, it may be programmed just once as a subroutine. Three statements are associated with subroutines: GOSUB, RETURN, and STOP.

```
10 DEF FNY(X) = X↑2-4
20 PRINT "1ST QUADRANT PLOT"
30 REM *** GET INFORMATION ABOUT X
40 PRINT "LARGEST X";
50 INPUT B
60 PRINT "X INCREMENT";
70 INPUT C
80 REM *** FIND LARGEST Y & ASSIGN TO M
90 LET M = -999999
100 FOR X=0 TO B STEP C
110 IF FNY(X)<M THEN 130
120 LET M = FNY(X)
130 NEXT X
140 REM *** INCREASE M TO INTEGER DIVISIBLE BY 50
150 LET M = 50*(INT(M/50)+1)
160 PRINT "LARGEST Y = "; M
170 IF M<=0 THEN 380
180 REM *** COMPUTE SCALE FACTOR
190 LET K = 50/M
200 PRINT "Y INCREMENT = "; 1/K
210 REM *** PRINT Y-AXIS
220 FOR I=0 TO 50
230 PRINT ".";
240 NEXT I
250 PRINT "Y"
260 REM *** PRINT X-AXIS & GRAPH
270 FOR X=C TO B STEP C
280 LET Y = FNY(X)
290 IF Y<0 THEN 350
300 IF Y=0 THEN 330
310 PRINT "."; TAB(K*Y); "*"
320 GOTO 360
330 PRINT "*"
340 GOTO 360
350 PRINT "."
360 NEXT X
370 PRINT "X"
380 END

RUN
1ST QUADRANT PLOT
LARGEST X? 10
X INCREMENT? 1
LARGEST Y =   100
Y INCREMENT =   2
..................................................Y
.
*
. *
.     *
.        *
.           *
.              *
.                 *
.                    *
.                       *
.                          *
X
```

```
# GOSUB line-number

    Execute line-number next and con-
    tinue until RETURN statement.
```

```
# RETURN

    Return from subroutine to main
    program. Continue at line follow-
    ing GOSUB.
```

```
# STOP   Terminate program execution.
```

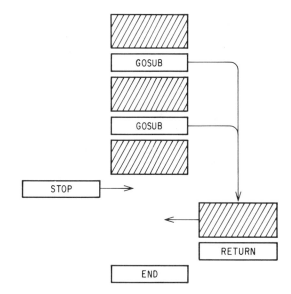

Fig. 9-3. Subroutine placement

To create a subroutine, the job or program is broken up into tasks (see Step 3 at the beginning of this chapter). If a particular task must be done several times, it can become a subroutine, and its position in the sequence is replaced by GOSUB. The task is then programmed once and inserted after the main program. The STOP statement is placed at the end of the main program, just before the subroutine. The END statement is placed, as usual, at the end of all statements. GOSUB and RETURN insure the proper sequence. The subroutine, programmed just once, will be performed every time it is "called" by GOSUB. The program in Fig. 9–3 might look something like this:

```
10 REM *** MAIN PROGRAM

• • •

100 GOSUB 400
110 REM *** CONTINUE MAIN PROGRAM

• • •

200 GOSUB 400
210 REM *** CONTINUE MAIN PROGRAM

• • •

300 STOP
400 REM *** SUBROUTINE BEGINS

• • •

490 RETURN
500 END
```

The subroutine, which starts in line 400, is called by line 100. Each statement in the subroutine is performed until RETURN appears. The program then continues at line 110. The program repeats the subroutine procedure when it encounters line 200. Upon returning at line 210, the main program continues until it reaches STOP.

A program may have more than one subroutine, and different people may write different sections of the program. One person can write the main program, which calls the subroutines in proper order and ends with STOP. Other people can write the subroutines, which begin at agreed-upon line numbers and end with RETURN. Whoever puts all the pieces together will provide the END statement. Most important, programmers must decide in advance which variables will represent the quantities used in the program.

For example, suppose that you have to find the greatest common factor (or GCF) of any three integers. Someone else has already solved this problem for any two integers, as shown at the top of the next page.

In this program, the variables have already been identified. Lines 100 through 170 receive two numbers in N and D and produce the GCF in D. Lines 10 through 40 and 200 through 210 are merely input and output.

Since the algorithm applies to only two numbers, we must use it twice. Having found the GCF of two integers, we can then find the GCF of the previous GCF and the third integer. This operation is shown in Fig. 9–4. The task which appears twice will be the subroutine. It occurs in lines 200 through 280 of the final solution, shown at the bottom of the next page. Compare these with lines 100 through 170 of the previous program. Also, in the final program, why did the programmer use GOTO instead of GOSUB in lines 70 and 130?

```
10 REM *** GET D & N (D<N) TO FIND THEIR GCF.
20 PRINT "INPUT NUMBERS, SMALLEST FIRST"
30 INPUT D
40 INPUT N
100 REM *** EUCLIDEAN ALGORITHM
110 LET Q = INT(N/D)
120 LET R = N-Q*D
130 IF R=0 THEN 170
140 LET N = D
150 LET D = R
160 GOTO 110
170 REM *** HERE, THE GCF = D.
200 PRINT "THE GCF IS "; D
210 END
```

```
10 REM *** FIND GCF OF ANY THREE INTEGERS.
20 PRINT "ENTER INTEGERS";
30 INPUT A, B, C
40 IF A>B THEN 80
50 LET N = B
60 LET D = A
70 GOTO 100
80 LET N = A
90 LET D = B
100 GOSUB 200
110 IF D>C THEN 140
120 LET N = C
130 GOTO 160
140 LET N = D
150 LET D = C
160 GOSUB 200
170 PRINT "THE GCF IS "; D
180 STOP
200 REM *** EUCLIDEAN ALGORITHM SUBROUTINE
210 LET Q = INT(N/D)
220 LET R = N-Q*D
230 IF R=0 THEN 270
240 LET N = D
250 LET D = R
260 GOTO 210
270 REM *** HERE, THE GCF = D.
280 RETURN
300 END
```

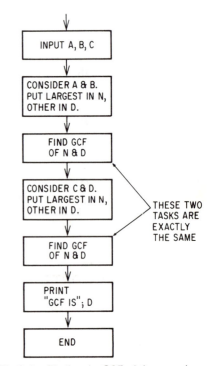

Fig. 9–4. Finding the GCF of three numbers

Problems

PLOTTING

Modify the "First Quadrant" plotting program so that it will accommodate three functions at once.

NOTES: You will have to sort the function values when plotting each line. Use a subroutine.

REPEAT

Write a program which will find the Greatest Common Factor of any list of integers.

NOTES: Your program can save the computer some work in this problem.   If at any point the GCF becomes 1, the rest of the list need not be processed.

CRYPTOGRAPHY

Spies who crack secret codes are often interested in which letters of a language appear most frequently. Using a text that you select from any novel in English write a program to count the number of times each of the characters (A-Z, 0-9, blank, and punctuation) appears in a sample of 1000 characters. Also tally the length of words (that is, the number of letters between successive blanks or punctuations). Also find the frequency of all ordered letter pairs—CH, HC, etc.—accumulating these in a matrix:

		Preceding letter				
		A	B	C	D	. . .
Succeeding letter	A					
	B					
	C					
	D					
	. . .					

For example, BASIC produces the pairs, BA, AS, SI, IC.

NOTES: Remember to print out your results in an appropriate format. For each preceding letter in the final matrix, do some succeeding letters appear more frequently than others?

SINE AND COSINE LAWS

In trigonometry, a common problem is to find all the sides and angles of a triangle, given any three of them. There are six possibilities for the "givens":

1. Three sides
2. Two sides and an angle between them
3. Two sides and an angle not between them
4. Two angles and a side between them
5. Two angles and a side not between them
6. Three angles.

Write a program to find all the sides and angles of any triangle, given the conditions described above. Angles should be input and printed in degrees, rather than radians.

POINTED TRIANGLES

Write a program which, given the coordinates (x,y) of any three points, will tell whether the points are collinear. If they are not collinear, the program should state that they are the vertices of a triangle and should identify that triangle as being either acute (all angles less than 90°), right (one angle equal to 90°), or obtuse (one angle greater than 90°). Also compute the area enclosed by the triangle and the lengths of the legs.

MEAN GRADES

A teacher has asked for help in grading test scores. You will be given a list of student names (not in alphabetic order) and a test score for each student. Write and test a program which will assign letter grades, and report the student names (in alphabetic order), their test scores, and their grades. The program should then report how many students were given an A, how many were given a B, and so forth.

Assign grades as follows, where m is the mean score and d is the standard deviation:

if	$m+d \leq score$	then grade is	A
	$m \leq score < m+d$		B
	$m-d \leq score < m$		C
	$m-2d \leq score < m-d$		D
	$score < m-2d$		F

NOTES: To find the "mean," do the following:

1. *Enter all the scores.*
2. *Find the sum of all scores.*
3. *Count how many scores there are.*
4. *The mean is the sum divided by the number of scores.*

To find the "standard deviation," do the following:

1. *From each score, subtract the mean (the difference is called the "deviation" of each score from the mean).*
2. *Square each deviation.*
3. *Find the sum of all squared deviations.*
4. *Divide this sum by the number of scores.*
5. *The standard deviation is the square root of this quotient.*

LITERARY DETECTIVE

Write a program which will measure the mean (average) word length, mean sentence length, and the standard deviation of each in a text of about 200 words in length. The program should do this given only the text, typed at the computer terminal.

Run the program on sections of two novels written by different authors. Does one author use longer words or sentences? There will be differences between almost all authors. Discuss the results with your teacher.

NOTES: See the notes for "Mean Grades" (this chapter).

MORTGAGES

Repayment of a home mortgage requires equal monthly payments. The amount of each payment, P, in dollars, is given by the following equation:

$$P = iA \left[\frac{(1 + i)^n}{(1 + i)^n - 1} \right]$$

where i is the monthly interest rate expressed as a decimal, A is the total amount of the mortgage in dollars, and n is the total number of monthly payments.

In any month, part of the payment is interest on the loan, and part repays the principal of the mortgage. If B is the remaining balance of the mortgage, the amount of a month's payment for interest (C) is

$$C = iB$$

while the amount credited to paying off the loan (D) is

$$D = P - iB$$

Usually, the buyer determines how much he needs to borrow. The lender knows the current interest rate and may offer repayment periods of 20, 25, or 30 years.

Write a program which will compute and print the monthly payments for a mortgage, when given the amount, the interest rate (expressed as a percent), and the repayment period (in years). The program should print (in columns) the amount of each payment, the part of each payment which is interest, and the part which pays off the loan. It should also total each of these columns.

In addition, the program should report the amount added to each monthly payment and to the total interest cost for:

1. An extra $5000 added to or removed from the loan
2. An extra one-half percent added to or removed from the interest rate
3. An extra five years added to or removed from the life of the mortgage.

These should be printed as simple numbers, not in columns. (Such information would allow the consumer to choose appropriate terms for his mortgage.)

NOTES: Typical input might be a loan of $35,000 for 25 years at 8½ percent interest.

NIM

Write a program which will play the game of Nim with a user. Nim is a two-player strategic game which originated in China thousands of years ago. Fifteen pebbles (or toothpicks or what-have-you) are placed in three piles, the first having seven pebbles, the second having five, and the third having three. Two players alternately take one, two, or three pebbles from the piles. The pebbles removed by one player in a turn must all be from the same pile. The player who takes the last pebble wins.

Like "One Pile," Nim has a winning strategy. This was derived in 1901, and it goes like this:

1. Convert the number of pebbles in each pile to binary.
2. Add each binary column separately (decimal addition will do).
3. Since the game is won by removing pebbles so as to leave an even sum in every column, proceed as follows:
   (a) Working from left (highest power of 2) to right, find the first column which has an odd sum.
   (b) Find a pile which has a binary 1 in this column.
   (c) Remove pebbles from this pile until the sums become all even.

For example, at the start of the game, the situation is as follows:

	Number of pebbles (decimal)		Number of pebbles (binary)		
First pile	7	=	1	1	1
Second pile	5	=	1	0	1
Third pile	3	=	0	1	1
Decimal sum			2	2	3

The first player can start a winning pattern by removing one counter from any pile so as to leave an even sum in the third column. What move should a player make if all sums are even?

NOTES: See the problems "One Pile" (Chap. 7) and "Decimal To Binary" (Chap. 6) for hints.

Chapter 10
Introduction to Simulation

A flowchart shows what steps a computer must follow to perform a task. Flowcharts may also show the steps to be followed in doing something else, for example, operating an elevator. This kind of flowchart, representing a real process, may be called a "model." The real process will be called a "system." Programming a model and running it on a computer is called "simulation" (see Fig. 10–1). "To simulate" means to imitate or duplicate.

A model is something that behaves like the real thing. When the model's equations and decisions are coded in the form of a program, the program causes the computer to imitate the system. The simulation is run in order to understand or foresee how the real process will behave whenever the real process is

1. Not well understood (for example, the effects of pollution).
2. Too time-consuming to observe (for example, population growth over many generations).
3. Too expensive to do more than once (for example, a space mission).
4. Too dangerous to observe (for example, a fire spreading through a building).
5. Involved with something that requires trial-and-error to do properly (an assembly line).

Systems that have been simulated include airports, warehouses, banks, hospitals, libraries, post offices, telephone networks, factories, mines, cities, countries, forests, and animal communities. In each case, the simulation was performed to duplicate the operation, processing, or growth of certain elements of the system. These might be traffic, money, communications, freight, services, jobs, machines, population levels, or natural resources. As you can see, simulation has a wide variety of uses.

Simulation with time not a variable

The easiest simulations are those which do not involve time as a variable. Programs which imitate coin tossing, dice throwing, or card playing fall into this category. Such programs do involve probability. The outcome of each event in the simulation—say, the roll of a die—is determined by a random number.

Suppose that we want to write a program which will simulate 1000 throws of two dice. On one throw of two dice, it is possible to obtain a total from 2 to 12. Simply generating a random integer from 2 to 12 will not solve our problem, however, because the chances of all outcomes are not the same. There are more ways to make a total of 7 than there are ways to make any other total (see Table 10–1).

Table 10–1   Calculated probabilities for one throw of two dice

Total of two dice	Number of ways to make each total	Probability of each total
2 or 12	1	0.028
3 or 11	2	0.056
4 or 10	3	0.083
5 or 9	4	0.111
6 or 8	5	0.139
7	6	0.166

To do this simulation, a program will have to generate two random integers, both from 1 to 6, and add them. Each integer represents the outcome of throwing one die. Rather than print the result of each throw, our program will tally all 1000 throws of two dice. Note that the distribution of "actual" throws closely resembles the distribution of probabilities, as one would expect.

```
5 DIM C(12)
10 FOR I=2 TO 12
15 LET C(I) = 0
20 NEXT I
25 PRINT "1000 THROWS OF TWO DICE"
```

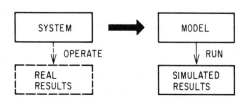

Fig. 10-1. Simulation

```
30 FOR N=1 TO 1000
40 LET D1 = INT(6*RND(0)+1)
50 LET D2 = INT(6*RND(0)+1)
60 LET T = D1+D2
70 LET C(T) = C(T)+1
80 NEXT N
90 PRINT "TOTAL", "NUMBER"
95 PRINT "OF DICE", "OF TIMES"
100 PRINT "-------", "--------"
110 FOR T=2 TO 12
120 PRINT T, C(T)
130 NEXT T
140 END

RUN
1000 THROWS OF TWO DICE
TOTAL           NUMBER
OF DICE         OF TIMES
-------         --------
   2               39
   3               53
   4               94
   5              115
   6              120
   7              175
   8              122
   9              117
  10               90
  11               57
  12               18

READY
```

As indicated in this example, one must be careful when the chance of each outcome is not the same. In such cases, a "Monte Carlo" method can be used. In this method, the random number is not the outcome (as it was above) but is used to determine the outcome.

Suppose that we are to simulate sales at a used car lot. We have been told that the probability is 0.4 that a sale will be made, and 0.6 that a sale will not be made on any day. On a particular day, how should the computer simulate a sale or no sale? It can be done by obtaining a random integer from zero to nine. If the integer is zero, one, two, or three, then a sale is made. If the integer is from four to nine, then a sale is not made. As required, we have four chances out of ten to make a sale. Note that the random integer itself is not the outcome.

Simulation involving time

In the example of throwing two dice, the program behaved as though one pair of dice were thrown 1000 times. Each pass through the program ended when the result of that throw was tallied. If we had "thrown" 1000 pairs of dice all at once, however, the results would have been the same. The 1000 events are independent.

In simulations involving time, each pass through the program ends when the events associated with that time are finished. Later events depend on what happened earlier, in one of two ways:

1. Changes in the system occur at specific times that are far apart. An example is a supermarket checkout counter, minute by minute. Shoppers arrive or depart many minutes apart. Such a situation is handled by "discrete" simulation.

2. Changes in the system occur throughout regular intervals of time. An example is a city water supply, day by day. Each day, the level of the reservoir depends on the rate of consumption and the rainfall accumulated over the previous day. Such a situation is handled by "continuous" simulation.

What a system does will determine which simulation is used. System processes differ in each case. A "process" is an activity performed by the system. Whenever a process starts, changes, or stops is called an "event."

Discrete simulation is concerned with specific things which are processed by the system and with things which do the processing. In discrete simulation, time is advanced from event to event, as shown by the example in the next section.

Continuous simulation is concerned with the total amounts or "levels" of things in a system. It also involves the "rates" at which these levels change over periods of time. In continuous simulation, there are no events. The value of time is advanced in identical small steps (as in a clock). At each step, we determine how system levels and rates have changed since the last step.

Discrete simulation

In the case of discrete simulation, the model is a flowchart which shows how the system handles events. The model must generate future events and store them in an "event list." At each step, the program will advance to the next event in the list.

The model must allow for both "independent" and "conditional" events. In a machine shop, for instance, an independent event would be the arrival of a new job. Such an event has no relation to what the system is currently doing. If all machines are busy, the new job would be placed in a "queue" or waiting line. A conditional event, on the other hand, would be putting a job on a machine. Such

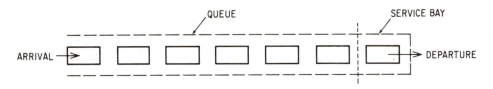

Fig. 10-2. Queueing

an event depends on a machine being idle and on a job being available in the queue.

Independent events will be simulated with probability (just as we simulated throwing dice). Conditional events will depend on the state of the system.

For example, suppose "Speedy's Auto Repair" is about to build a store in a small town. They know from experience that customers arrive at random, up to 120 minutes apart. They also know that jobs require from 15 to 90 minutes of work. Will one service bay be enough? The system actually looks like Fig. 10-2.

When simulating the system, we will measure both the average service time (from arrival to completion) and the length of the queue at the arrival of each customer. The events in this system consist of arrivals and departures. A model of the system appears in Fig. 10-3. Before writing a program, however, we must identify some variables (remember to follow the steps listed in the previous chapter).

The "event list" (Fig. 10-4) will be E(I). Each item in the list represents a future event. Each number in E(I) is the time at which an event will occur. A departure corresponds to E(1); there can be only one scheduled departure. If E(1) is 999999, then the service bay is empty. Arrival times are in E(2) through E(9). The variable P will indicate the current event, E(P). A variable used this way is called a "pointer."

The "queue" will be Q(J). Each item represents a customer or job waiting. Each number in Q(J) is the time at which the job arrived. The service bay is Q(1). If Q(1) is zero, then the service bay is empty. Waiting jobs are in Q(2) through Q(9). With each job is a service time, listed in S(J). The variable L will indicate the length of the queue. Q(L) is the last job in the queue.

The current time is T. For record keeping, Y(L) will hold the number of times that the queue was L jobs long. This is tallied whenever a customer arrives. The total of all service times is X, and the number of jobs completed is N. When the simulation is finished, then X/N will be the average service time per customer. The entire program appears on the next two pages. It will run until 100 "jobs" have been completed.

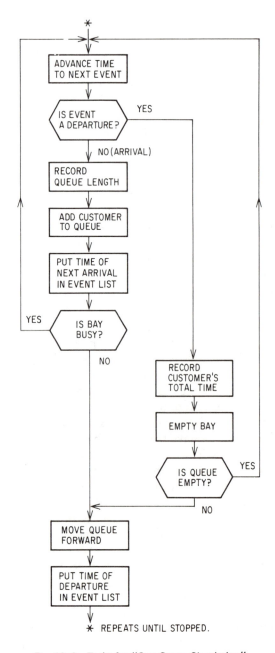

Fig. 10-3. Tasks for "One Queue Simulation"

The BASIC Workbook

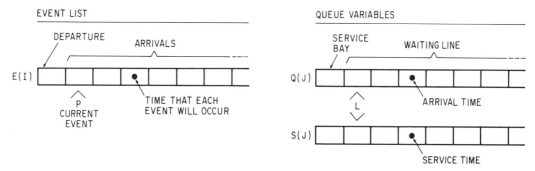

EVENT LIST

DEPARTURE   ARRIVALS

E(I)

P
CURRENT
EVENT

TIME THAT EACH
EVENT WILL OCCUR

QUEUE VARIABLES

SERVICE
BAY   WAITING LINE

Q(J)

L

ARRIVAL TIME

S(J)

SERVICE TIME

Fig. 10-4. Simulation variables

```
10 PRINT "ONE QUEUE SIMULATION"
20 DIM E(9), Q(9), S(9), Y(9)
30 FOR I=1 TO 9
40    LET E(I) = 999999
50 NEXT I
60 REM *** START WITH AN ARRIVAL EVENT
70 LET P = 2
80 LET E(P) = T+INT(105*RND(0)+16)
100 REM *** FIND NEXT EVENT
110 LET P = 1
120 FOR I=2 TO 9
130    IF E(P)<E(I) THEN 150
140    LET P = I
150 NEXT I
160 REM *** ADVANCE TIME
170 LET T = E(P)
180 REM *** SKIP IF EVENT IS DEPARTURE
190 IF P=1 THEN 400
200 REM *** EVENT IS ARRIVAL
205 REM *** RECORD LENGTH OF QUEUE
210 LET Y(L) = Y(L)+1
220 REM *** PLACE ARRIVAL IN QUEUE
230 IF L>0 THEN 250
240 LET L = 1
250 LET L = L+1
260 LET Q(L) = T
270 LET S(L) = INT(75*RND(0)+16)
300 REM *** PLACE NEXT ARRIVAL IN EVENT LIST
310 LET E(P) = T+INT(120*RND(0)+1)
320 REM *** RETURN IF SERVICE BAY IS BUSY
330 IF Q(1)<>0 THEN 100
340 GOTO 500
400 REM *** EVENT IS DEPARTURE
405 REM *** RECORD TOTAL TIME
410 LET X = X+(T-Q(1))
420 LET N = N+1
430 REM *** EMPTY BAY & REMOVE SCHEDULED DEPARTURE
440 LET Q(1) = 0
450 LET S(1) = 0
460 LET E(1) = 999999
470 REM *** RETURN IF QUEUE EMPTY
480 IF Q(2)=0 THEN 100
```

Introduction to Simulation

```
500 REM *** MOVE QUEUE
510 FOR J=1 TO L
520     LET Q(J) = Q(J+1)
530     LET S(J) = S(J+1)
540 NEXT J
550 LET L = L-1
560 REM *** PUT DEPARTURE IN EVENT LIST
570 LET E(1) = T+S(1)
600 REM *** REPEAT FOR 100 CUSTOMERS
610 IF N<100 THEN 100
700 REM *** REPORT RESULTS
710 PRINT "CURRENT TIME IS "; T; " MINUTES."
715 PRINT "OR "; T/480; " WORKING DAYS."
720 PRINT "THERE WERE "; N; " CUSTOMERS."
730 PRINT "AVERAGE SERVICE TIME WAS "; X/N; " MIN."
740 PRINT "QUEUE LENGTHS WHEN JOBS ARRIVED:"
750 PRINT "LENGTH"; "FREQUENCY"
760 FOR L=0 TO 9
770     PRINT L, Y(L)
780 NEXT L
800 END
```

Problems

GROWING PAINS

One of the problems in Chapter 7, "Population Density," listed census populations for seventeen states. Use that data to write a program which will list, in five columns and with appropriate headings, the following items:

1. The years from 1790 to 1970 in differences of ten
2. The census population in each of these years
3. The ratio of each population figure to the previous one (to the nearest hundredth)
4. The value of P, where

$$P = \text{INT}(10X + 0.5)/10$$
$$X = Ne^{RT}$$
$$R = Ae^{-BT} + C$$
$$T = Y - 1790$$
$$Y = \text{the year (i.e., 1790, 1800, 1810, ...)}$$
$$N = 3.82$$
$$A = 0.0186$$
$$B = 0.00486$$
$$C = 0.00895$$

5. The ratio of each value of P to the previous one (to the nearest hundredth)

A set of equations which duplicates a set of actual values is called a "mathematical model." If the value of P accurately follows the real population trend, what would you expect the population to be in 1980? In 2030?

What historical factors might have influenced the rate of population growth in these seventeen states over the years? Can you find any evidence in the ratios of actual populations?

STOCK MARKET

Write a program which will simulate the random price fluctuations of a stock market.

In every day's trading, the probability that the market will continue the previous day's trend (rising or falling) is 0.75, and the probability that it will reverse the trend is 0.25.

If the market continues the previous trend, the amount of change in the price index is a random integer between zero and 25. If the trend is reversed, the change is a random integer between zero and 100.

The market opens with a price index of 250 and a rising trend. Generate the index each day for thirty days. Use a "1st Quadrant Plotter" with a maximum Y value of 500 to chart the month's activity. The price index will be the Y-axis, and the days will fall on the X-axis. Do all of this in one program.

MILLION MONKEYS

An old story concerns the probability that a monkey might produce a Shakespearean sonnet if he were one of a million monkeys seated at typewriters and typing letters at random. (It's not likely.)

PART I: Have the computer print 1000 random letters, each of the 26 letters having an equal chance of appearing. Your program should print one letter at a time and use a trailing semicolon to fill each line (save paper). Run the program three times. How many separate (not overlapping) words of two or more letters can you find in each printout?

PART II: Your results from Part I will contain few words, because in English the chances of letter's appearing are not equal. Modify your program so that letters appear with the frequency that they do in English. Run this program three times. Compared with the results from Part I, are more words formed and are longer words formed?

NOTES: Do both parts of this problem. In English, letters appear approximately as follows:

Letter	Frequency of each
E	13 %
A H I N O R S T	7 %
C D L M U	3 %
B F G P W Y	2 %
J K Q V	1 %
X Z	—

SPEEDY SPEEDY

After opening the store with one queue (see text), "Speedy's Auto Repair" discovered that things did not turn out as planned. Jobs do not require from 15 to 90 minutes of work. The amount of work required is actually of two types:

1. Type A makes up 60 percent of the jobs and requires from 15 to 45 minutes of work.
2. Type B makes up 40 percent of the jobs and requires from 45 to 120 minutes of work.

Simulate this situation for 100 jobs, measuring the average time required per job and tallying the length of the queue. Assume that Speedy continues to service first that job which arrived first in the queue. Then suppose that Speedy has an idea to reduce the waiting time. The bay will service first that job in the queue which requires the least work time. Simulate this situation for 100 jobs. Would you recommend that Speedy adopt this policy or stay with the old way of "first in, first out"?

TRAFFIC LIGHTS

In the middle of a busy one-way street, there is a pedestrian walkway. Vehicle traffic and pedestrian crossings are regulated by a traffic light. In every ten seconds, a random number of vehicles, between 5 and 20, arrive at the intersection. Up to 20 cars can cross the intersection in ten seconds if the light in their direction is green. In ten seconds, a random number of pedestrians, between zero and 40, arrive at the walkway. Up to 30 pedestrians can cross in ten seconds if the light in their direction is green.

Write a program which will simulate this intersection for a period of ten minutes if the light is set at X seconds green for vehicles and 60 – X seconds green for pedestrians. Measure the total waiting time for pedestrians and the total waiting time for vehicles. (Total waiting time is the number of pedestrians or vehicles waiting multiplied by the period of time that they wait.)

Then run your program so that it simulates ten minutes for each of the following light settings:

Setting	A	B	C	D	E
Pedestrian green	10	20	30	40	50
Vehicle green	50	40	30	20	10

What would be the best timing for the lights? Would you recommend a cycle longer than 60 seconds?

NOTES: This problem should be solved without arrays.

RANDOM WORDS

If you have already solved the "Million Monkeys" problem (this chapter), you may do either Part I or Part II of this problem.

PART I: Start with a program which prints random letters with the frequency with which they appear in English. If spaces were inserted so as to form random-length words, what should the frequency of a space be? Does adding spaces decrease the number of real words formed? (See the results of "Literary Detective," Chapter 9, for hints.)

PART II: Start with a program which prints random letters with the frequency with which they appear in English. Should the probability of a letter appearing depend on the letter just printed? For instance, should the probability of an H be greater than 7 out of 100 if the letter just printed was C or S or T? Write a program which will print 1000 random letters, varying the probability as just described. Does this increase the number of real words formed? (See the results of "Cryptography," Chapter 9, for hints.)

LIFE

The issues of *Scientific American* for October 1970, February 1971, and January 1972 introduced a game invented by John Horton Conway and called "Life."

On a grid, assume that a neighborhood consists of the eight elements surrounding any given element (see Fig. 10-5). Also assume that at any time, an element will be "alive" if either (1) it was "alive" at the previous time, and exactly two or three of its neighbors were also alive, or (2) it was blank at the previous time, and exactly three of its neighbors were alive. Otherwise, an element will be blank at that time.

Write a program which will simulate the changes in a 17 × 17 grid, over 15 units of time, printing the whole grid as it appears in each unit of time. Use an asterisk (*) to denote an element that is alive.

Then run the program three times, with the following elements initially alive in the center of the grid:

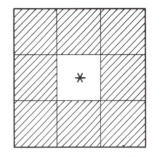

Fig. 10-5. Shaded area is the neighborhood of the asterisk

First: (7,8), (8,9), (9,9), (9,8), (9,7)
Second: (8,9), (9,8), (9,9), (9,10)
Third: (7,7), (7,8), (7,9), (7,10), (7,11), (8,10), (9,9), (10,8), (11,7), (11,8), (11,9), (11,10), (11,11)

The numbers here are (R,C) where R is the row from top to bottom and C is the column from left to right, in a 17 × 17 matrix.

NOTES: This problem requires two matrices, one to represent the state of the system at the current time, and the other to represent the state of the system at the previous time. With each pass through the program, time advances one unit, the current grid becomes the previous grid, and a new current grid is computed and printed.

This is not an easy program to write. Care should be taken to find a solution that requires the fewest numbers of computations.

Appendix A
Summary of Minimal Basic

Elements

Constants	Numbers or characters
Variables (v)	Single letter, or single letter followed by single digit
	Single letter with single or double subscript
	Single letter followed by $
Operations	Algebraic ($\uparrow$ * / + –) and functions
Expressions (e)	Numbers and/or numeric variables separated by operations (parentheses may be used)
Relations (r)	$<$ $<=$ $=$ $>=$ $>$ $<>$
Line numbers (# or i)	Integers

Program statements

# DATA n_1, n_2	Values for variables in READ
# DEF FNa(v) = e	Defines a function named FNa
# DIM $v_1(n_1)$, $v_2(n_2, n_3)$	Reserves n locations for array
# END	Terminates program execution
# FOR v = e_1 TO e_2 STEP e_3	Does all statements between FOR and NEXT for each value of v starting at e_1 through e_2 increased by e_3 each time
# GOSUB i	Executes line i next and continues until RETURN
# GOTO i	Continues execution at line i
# IF e_1 r e_2 THEN i	If relation between expressions is true, then continue at line i. If relation is false, continue at line following this one.
# INPUT v_1, v_2	Gets values of variables from keyboard
# LET v = e	Assigns value of expression to variable
# NEXT v	Last statement in program loop
# ON e GOTO i_1, i_2, i_3	If INT(e+0.5)=1, then continue execution at line i_1. If INT(e+0.5)=2, then continue at line i_2, etc.
# PRINT e_1; e_2, "text"	Prints values of expressions and specified text. Spacing controlled by semicolon and comma.
# RANDOMIZE	Starts RND function at random
# READ v_1, v_2	Gets values of variables from DATA list
# REM text	Comment
# RESTORE	Starts READ at beginning of DATA list
# RETURN	Returns from subroutine to line following GOSUB
# STOP	Terminates program execution

Functions

SQR(X)	Square root of X
ABS(X)	Absolute value (magnitude) of X
SGN(X)	Sign of X: +1 if X is positive; 0 if X is zero; –1 if X is negative
INT(X)	Largest integer in X
SIN(X)	Sine of X radians
COS(X)	Cosine of X radians
TAN(X)	Tangent of X radians

ATN(X)	Arctangent of X (angle in radians whose tangent is X)
EXP(X)	e^X
LOG(X)	$\log_e X$
RND or RND(X)	Random number between 0 and 1
TAB(X)	Controls location of printing head

Appendix B
Correcting Mistakes at the Terminal

RUBOUT

While typing a line (before pressing the carriage return key), typing a RUBOUT or ←
nullifies the character just typed. Pressing RUBOUT twice deletes two characters, and so
forth. (RUBOUT is SHIFT/O on some machines.)

Retype line

Simply retyping a line replaces the line with the same line number previously stored
in memory.

Insert line

Typing a line numbered j inserts that line between lines with numbers i and k currently
stored in memory, where i<j<k.

Remove line

On some systems, typing a line number and pressing the RETURN key erases the line
with that line number previously stored in memory. On other systems, this is accomplished
with a system command, "DELETE line number."

The mysterious unending program

On occasion, some programs look correct but refuse to terminate. For example:

```
10 LET X = X+.1
20 IF X=2 THEN 50
30 PRINT X
40 GOTO 10
50 PRINT "ALL DONE"
60 END
```

This program will usually not terminate because of "round-off error." This is a characteristic of the computer, not a fault of the programmer's logic. Just as irrationals cannot be
expressed in decimal numbers, fractions are misrepresented by the binary numbers used in
computers. In a computer, 0.1 is a number slightly less than that. So, in line 20 above,
X will never exactly equal two. The solution to this problem has the form of a rule: Unless
the values are known to be integers, test for inequality. For example, rewrite line 20 above
to say:

```
20 IF X>=2 THEN 50
```

Tracing

Tracing is a method used to locate program bugs. It consists of adding extra PRINT statements when the program is tested. These statements show the values of intermediate quantities used in calculations. After testing, trace statements are removed to leave the program in its final, debugged form.

Trace statements are especially helpful in loops. An extra print statement inside the loop can show how many times the loop is executed and what the changing values are. It is a common error to execute a loop one too few or one too many times.

Appendix C
More About Plotters

An adjustment

In the plotting program shown in Chap. 9, one important step was

```
140 REM *** INCREASE M TO INTEGER DIVISIBLE BY 50
150 LET M = 50*(INT(M/50)+1)
```

This establishes an evenly divisible upper bound for the Y-axis. However, it also yields a plotter which will not work for very small functions (M<5). To handle all cases, we must be able to expand and shrink the Y scale, as follows:

	If largest Y is			*Then replace M by an integer multiple of*
100	< M <	1000	. . .	50
10	< M <	100	. . .	5
1	< M <	10	. . .	.5
.1	< M <	1	. . .	.05

This means that line 150 should be replaced by two lines. The first sets the order of magnitude:

```
150 LET Q = 5*10↑INT(LOG(M)/LOG(10)-1)
```

The second replaces the largest value of Y to be plotted with an integer multiple of Q:

```
155 LET M = Q*(INT(M/Q)+1)
```

These will both compress and expand the scale, depending on the range of the function to be plotted.

Positive X plotter; fixed X-axis

By modifying the "1st Quadrant Plotter" shown in Chap. 9, negative values of Y can be accommodated. Such a "Positive X Plotter" appears below. It will always print the X-axis at a "fixed" position, in the center of the page, even if it is run with a different function or with different values of B and C (largest X and X-increment).

You may want to compare this program with the "1st Quadrant Plotter" and note the changes that have been made.

```
10 DEF FNY(X) = X↑2-4
20 PRINT "POSITIVE X PLOTTER, FIXED X-AXIS"
30 REM *** GET INFORMATION ABOUT X
40 PRINT "LARGEST X";
50 INPUT B
60 PRINT "X INCREMENT";
70 INPUT C
```

```
80 REM *** FIND LARGEST ABS(Y) & ASSIGN TO M
90 LET M = -999999
100 FOR X=0 TO B STEP C
110 IF ABS(FNY(X))<M THEN 130
120 LET M = ABS(FNY(X))
130 NEXT X
140 REM *** INCREASE M TO INTEGER DIVISIBLE BY 25
150 LET M = 25*(INT(M/25)+1)
160 PRINT "LARGEST Y = "; M
170 IF M<=0 THEN 380
180 REM *** COMPUTE SCALE FACTOR
190 LET K = 25/M
200 PRINT "Y INCREMENT = "; 1/K
210 REM *** PRINT Y-AXIS
220 FOR I=0 TO 50
230 PRINT ".";
240 NEXT I
250 PRINT "Y"
260 REM *** PRINT X-AXIS & GRAPH
270 FOR X=C TO B STEP C
280 LET Y = FNY(X)
290 IF Y<0 THEN 350
300 IF Y=0 THEN 330
310 PRINT TAB(25); "."; TAB(25+K*Y); "*"
320 GOTO 360
330 PRINT TAB(25); "*"
340 GOTO 360
350 PRINT TAB(25+K*Y); "*"; TAB(25); "."
360 NEXT X
370 PRINT TAB(25); "X"
380 END

RUN
POSITIVE X PLOTTER, FIXED X-AXIS
LARGEST X? 10
X INCREMENT? 1
LARGEST Y =  100
Y INCREMENT =  4
..................................................Y
                         *.
                         *
                         .*
                         .   *
                         .     *
                         .       *
                         .         *
                         .           *
                         .             *
                         .               *
                         X

READY
```

Positive X plotter; floating X-axis

The plotter with a fixed X-axis may not be altogether satisfactory, because it does not use the full width of the page for the graph. Also, it does not show the Y-intercept.

Both of these features can be included in a plotter which prints the X-axis at a variable position across the page. The position of the X-axis will depend on the function and the range of values to be plotted. This "floating" X-axis will enable the graph of the function to be spread across the width of the page.

In this program, we need to determine the largest value of Y and the smallest value of Y over the domain of X. If the Y-axis is to be 50 spaces long, the scale factor will be:

$$K = \frac{50}{\text{Largest Y} - \text{Smallest Y}}$$

If the smallest Y is greater than zero, or the largest Y is less than zero, then the X-axis must appear on the left or the right side of the page.

The plotting program with a floating X-axis appears below. The primary tasks (indicated by REM statements) differ significantly from the two previous plotters.

```
10 DEF FNY(X) = X↑2-4
20 PRINT "POSITIVE X PLOTTER, FLOATING X-AXIS"
30 REM *** GET INFORMATION ABOUT X
40 PRINT "LARGEST X";
50 INPUT B
60 PRINT "X INCREMENT";
70 INPUT C
80 REM *** FIND S=SMALLEST Y, L=LARGEST Y
90 LET S = 999999
100 LET L = -999999
110 FOR X=0 TO B STEP C
120 LET Y = FNY(X)
130 IF Y>S THEN 150
140 LET S = Y
150 IF Y<L THEN 170
160 LET L = Y
170 NEXT X
180 REM *** NEED LEFT- OR RIGHT-SIDE AXIS?
190 IF SGN(S)<0 THEN 210
200 LET S = 0
210 IF SGN(L)>0 THEN 230
220 LET L = 0
230 REM *** MAKE WIDTH (L-S) DIVISIBLE BY 50
240 LET W = L-S
250 LET W = 50*INT((W/50)+1)
260 REM *** COMPUTE SCALE FACTOR
270 LET K = 50/W
280 PRINT "PLOTTED VALUES OF Y ARE FROM "; S; " TO "; L
285 PRINT "Y-AXIS INCREMENT IS "; 1/K
290 REM *** PRINT Y-AXIS & Y-INTERCEPT (P TAB)
300 LET P = INT((FNY(0)-S)*K)
310 FOR I=0 TO 49
320 IF I<>P THEN 340
330 PRINT "*";
340 PRINT ".";
350 NEXT I
360 PRINT "Y"
```

The BASIC Workbook
114

```
370 REM *** PRINT X-AXIS (V TAB) & GRAPH (P TAB)
380 LET V = INT(-S*K)
390 FOR X=C TO B STEP C
400 LET Y = FNY(X)
410 LET P = INT((Y-S)*K)
420 IF P<V THEN 480
430 IF P=V THEN 460
440 PRINT TAB(V); "."; TAB(P); "*"
450 GOTO 490
460 PRINT TAB(P); "*"
470 GOTO 490
480 PRINT TAB(P); "*"; TAB(V); "."
490 NEXT X
500 PRINT TAB(V); "X"
510 END


RUN
POSITIVE X PLOTTER, FLOATING X-AXIS
LARGEST X? 10
X INCREMENT? 1
PLOTTED VALUES OF Y ARE FROM -4  TO  96
Y-AXIS INCREMENT IS  2
*...............................................................Y
*  .
    *
  .  *
  .    *
  .      *
  .        *
  .          *
  .            *
  .              *
  .                *
  .                  *
  X
```

READY

Four-quadrant plotter

A general, four-quadrant plotter is a simple extension of the positive X plotter with a floating X-axis. The biggest difference is that values of X need not start with zero. Thus the user must be asked to provide the smallest value of X to be plotted.

In addition, previous programs plotted the Y-axis before the graph. This plotter, shown below, prints the Y-axis only when X is zero.

```
10 DEF FNY(X) = X↑2-4
20 PRINT "ONE FUNCTION PLOTTER, FLOATING X-AXIS"
30 REM *** GET INFORMATION ABOUT X
33 PRINT "SMALLEST X";
37 INPUT A
40 PRINT "LARGEST X";
50 INPUT B
60 PRINT "X INCREMENT";
70 INPUT C
80 REM *** FIND S=SMALLEST Y, L=LARGEST Y
```

```
90 LET S = 999999
100 LET L = -999999
110 FOR X=A TO B STEP C
120 LET Y = FNY(X)
130 IF Y>S THEN 150
140 LET S = Y
150 IF Y<L THEN 170
160 LET L = Y
170 NEXT X
180 REM *** NEED LEFT- OR RIGHT-SIDE AXIS?
190 IF SGN(S)<0 THEN 210
200 LET S = 0
210 IF SGN(L)>0 THEN 230
220 LET L = 0
230 REM *** MAKE WIDTH (L-S) DIVISIBLE BY 50
240 LET W = L-S
250 LET W = 50*INT((W/50)+1)
260 REM *** COMPUTE SCALE FACTOR
270 LET K = 50/W
280 PRINT "PLOTTED VALUES OF Y ARE FROM "; S; " TO "; L
285 PRINT "Y-AXIS INCREMENT IS "; 1/K
290 REM *** START PLOTTING
300 REM *** SET TABS FOR X-AXIS (V TAB) & GRAPH (P TAB)
310 LET V = INT(-S*K)
320 FOR X=A TO B STEP C
330 LET Y = FNY(X)
340 LET P = INT((Y-S)*K)
350 IF X<>0 THEN 430
360 REM *** IF X=0, PRINT Y-AXIS & Y-INTERCEPT (AT P)
370 FOR I=0 TO 49
380 IF I<>P THEN 400
390 PRINT "*";
400 PRINT ".";
410 NEXT I
420 PRINT "Y"
430 REM *** CONTINUE PLOTTING
440 REM *** PRINT X-AXIS (V TAB) & GRAPH (P TAB)
450 IF P<V THEN 510
460 IF P=V THEN 490
470 PRINT TAB(V); "."; TAB(P); "*"
480 GOTO 520
490 PRINT TAB(P); "*"
500 GOTO 520
510 PRINT TAB(P); "*"; TAB(V); "."
520 NEXT X
530 PRINT TAB(V); "X"
540 END

RUN
ONE FUNCTION PLOTTER, FLOATING X-AXIS
SMALLEST X? -4
LARGEST X? 6
X INCREMENT? 1
PLOTTED VALUES OF Y ARE FROM -4  TO  32
Y-AXIS INCREMENT IS  1
```

```
                        *
              *
           *
    *
* . . . . . . . . . . . . . . . . . . . . . . . . . . . . . . . . . . . . . . . . . . . . . . . Y
*
   *
      *
   *
      *
                 *
            *
                       *
                                 *
   X
```

`READY`

A final note about plotters

All the plotting programs which appear in this book have at least three limitations. First, they print the graph of only one function. Second, the function must be continuous. Third, the function must be analytic, that is, defined by an equation. Plotters can be written to store (x,y) points in subscripted variables, X(I) and Y(I), then plot those points. This approach allows nonanalytic functions to be displayed.

Index

119